Praise

When God Says, 'Wait'

"In *When God Says, 'Wait,'* Elizabeth captures readers through previously unexplored anecdotes of familiar Bible stories and then connects you with these ancient icons, venturing deeper into their narratives. With Elizabeth's own graceful confessions and by linking our own emotions to those of these past heroes, we internalize so much more than just the moral of their stories. We take on their hope, their insight, and their love for God in a way that helps us navigate this 'lonely, unmarked territory' that is waiting. We have known Elizabeth and her husband Kevin for many years. We value their guidance, direction, and most of all their genuine desire for a relationship with Christ. This book is the culmination of years of grappling with questions and faith-testing waiting with practical insights of the way God works in these times."

–Pauli and Chip Wade, Lead Creative at Wade Works,
Star of HGTV's "Elbow Room" and "Curb Appeal"

"Elizabeth Thompson is a kindred spirit. I love her writing style, heart, and quirky humor. She writes with authenticity and wisdom. *When God Says, 'Wait'* gives practical, biblical precepts, but it also unites our hearts with beloved biblical characters. Thompson masterfully paints scenes from these characters' lives in such a way, you feel you're there. Time is removed. Rather than biblical saints, they become people just like us. Their stories are ours. It's a must-read for anyone struggling with God's timetable. Healing, hopeful, and filled with grace to help us trust God as we wait on Him."

–Andy Lee, Author of *A Mary Like Me: Flawed Yet Called*

"*When God Says, 'Wait'* is a must-read. Elizabeth gives us confidence and courage in times of waiting, ensuring that we will be 'better because of the wait.' We are better because of this book, too! With solid scriptural advice, practical prompts, and unmatched wit, Elizabeth helps us find faith in times of uncertainty. Whether you're a mom, student, business owner, or wife, this book is for you!"

–Lara Casey Isaacson, Author of *Make It Happen*

"It's hard to be the example, but someone's gotta do it! Thank goodness it is Elizabeth—her journey through waiting, wit in expressing it, and wisdom to learn from it. This book is not only a beautiful testament of one woman's faith, but a reminder of the many Bible heroes who God told to wait. Oftentimes life leaves us in the gap between what is and what will be. Thank you, Elizabeth, for refining the gifts that can only be given as we wait. Those gifts and this book will be a gap-filler and hope-giver to women all over the world."

–Laura Whitaker, Executive Director,
Extra Special People, Inc.

"As Elizabeth writes, when speed is our cultural priority, 'wait' feels like a bad word. Thanks be to God that this does not have to be the case and that through *When God Says, 'Wait'* we can uncover a roadmap to prayerful, humble, practical, and hopeful waiting—even in the midst of heartbreaking trial! Any reader will feel indebted to Elizabeth's fearless take on the misconceptions of waiting, sharing from a deep well of scripture-rich wisdom. While most authors dealing with such tender topics may shy away from hard-to-swallow truths, Elizabeth guides, challenges, and encourages just like a best friend—with vulnerability and humor—so that your heart can fall deeper in love with a God who sees, hears, and cares."

–Marilisa Schachinger,
Founder and Event Planner, Martel Events

When God Says *wait*

Navigating life's *detours and delays*
without losing your faith,
your friends, or your mind

Elizabeth Laing Thompson

SHILOH RUN PRESS
An Imprint of Barbour Publishing, Inc.

Print ISBN 978-1-68322-012-1

eBook Editions:
Adobe Digital Edition (.epub) 978-1-68322-304-7
Kindle and MobiPocket Edition (.prc) 978-1-68322-308-5

Cover design: Faceout Studio, www.faceoutstudio.com

Published by Shiloh Run Press, an imprint of Barbour Publishing, Inc., P.O. Box 719, Uhrichsville, Ohio 44683, www.shilohrunpress.com.

Our mission is to publish and distribute inspirational products offering exceptional value and biblical encouragement to the masses.

 Member of the
Evangelical Christian
Publishers Association

Printed in the United States of America.

Dedication

For Kevin

"I was made and meant to look for you
and wait for you
and become yours forever."
–Robert Browning

Acknowledgments

When you pursue a writing career for thirteen years, you have a lot of people to thank.

Lysa TerKeurst has called writing a book "a sacred adventure with God," and what a sacred adventure this was! Every day spent writing was a day spent in constant communion with God. Thank You, Father, for trusting me with Your Word and with this message.

My husband, Kevin, did not blink when I announced that I wanted to become a writer. He has read every draft, loved every story, humored every angsty moment. He has flown me to conferences, bought me a laptop when I ran over mine by accident (long story), and viewed every dollar spent as investment, not expense. He has gladly given me permission to do what I love and be who I am. Thank you—I am so blessed to be yours.

Thanks to Cassidy, Blake, Avery, and Sawyer, for being you, my four spunky miracles.

I can't begin to describe the debt I owe my parents and family—they have read and critiqued and prayed and fasted and mourned and rejoiced with me. Thank you to Dad, Mom, David, Lisa, Jonathan, Talia, Alexandra, Jesse, and many of my aunts and uncles and cousins. Kevin's parents, Bill and Glenda, have always encouraged, always believed, and often wrangled kids so I could write.

My writing partner, Emma, knows what I want to say and how I want to say it better than I do. She has sacrificed sleep, work, vacation, and sanity to help me write this book and get it right. I never want to write without you, Emma. (Really, I never want to do anything without you—*parabatai* are meant to be together always.)

Many thanks to my agent, Jessica Kirkland, for taking risks and dreaming big and fighting hard. You make the writing life a spiritual venture.

I'm so thankful for the blessed friends who have fasted and encouraged and mailed emergency chocolate: Sara, Julie, Karen, Allison, Laura, Melissa, Jeanie, Heather, Katie, Mindi, and Stacey. You have made the journey—and life—a joy.

Thanks to the women in my church who have been so encouraging and supportive. Thank you for letting me borrow some of your stories to share.

I'm deeply thankful to everyone at Barbour for their outstanding work. Thank you to Kelly McIntosh for your positive spirit, gracious words, and excellent standards. You've made the publishing process a great experience. Thank you to Laura Weller for your first-rate work editing the book—special thanks for keeping my commas under control. Thank you to Shalyn Sattler and Mary Burns and the entire marketing team for your creativity and enthusiasm. Many thanks to Ashley Schrock, creative director, for making this book beautiful. I am grateful to Brigitta Nortker (who is no longer at Barbour), for believing in this project.

Thanks to my writers' group in Athens, Georgia—Emma, Gail, Muriel, and Susan—for sticking with me. Gail, thank you for talking me into going to a Christian writing conference when I was ready to give up—you changed my life!

Thanks to The Tenors for the music that kept me inspired and in the zone.

And of course, I have to thank the baristas at my Starbucks for keeping me happily caffeinated, for letting me hog the window seat, and for not looking at me weird when I got crazy-eyed and started swaying in my seat to "Hallelujah."

Contents

1
Wait Is a Four-Letter Word

Miriam's Story
No Ordinary Child

Based on Exodus 2:1–10

Miriam crouches at water's edge, bare knees quivering, thin legs scratched by reeds, heart aching as she listens to her baby brother wail from within a basket. She prays, pleading harder than she has ever prayed in her young life.

And just when she thinks she can no longer bear the baby's screams, she hears voices—women's voices—laughing and chattering in Egyptian. They are coming closer.

Hope and fear surge, lightning through her veins; her stomach roils, the earth tips sideways. *Don't faint*, Miriam commands herself. Drawing a shaky breath, she bites down on her fist so hard she draws blood. These Egyptians will either save her brother or drown him. Either way, she cannot make a sound. She inches back into a thicker patch of reeds.

A pretty Egyptian girl, not much older than Miriam, wearing the robes of a servant, steps forward and parts the reeds. She spots the basket. The baby cries again, his voice now hoarse, weak. This tiny cry is worse than the rest, a dagger to Miriam's heart. He is hungry.

The servant girl gasps, looks around, flaps helpless hands. At last she tiptoes forward to draw Miriam's brother out of the basket.

Miriam watches his tiny, fat feet kicking as his blanket—the blanket she herself made for him—slips off and falls into the mud. Her arms ache for the feel of his soft, chubby body; she can almost feel him cuddled up warm against her chest, where he belongs. But still she does not move, does not make a sound.

The servant girl, holding the infant awkwardly—away from her body, as if he is diseased—steps away from the water and calls out. Miriam recognizes a few words in the foreign tongue: *Baby. Hebrew.*

Her stomach writhes. She is going to be sick.

She can't watch.

She can't look away.

Slowly, she creeps along the riverbank after the girl, keeping herself hidden in the tall grass. The servant girl carries the boy—still kicking and squirming but no longer crying—to the group of women clustered at the edge of a shallow pool, giggling and gossiping as they wade in the water.

A tall woman, dressed in royal garb, steps forward. The laughing voices grow silent. Miriam's breath catches.

Pharaoh's daughter.

The servant girl lifts the baby up so the princess can see.

Kick, kick—fat baby feet dangle over the water.

Miriam's legs quake. Her teeth clamp down over her tongue, holding a scream inside. Her fingernails dig into dirt, holding her body down.

Time stops.

The princess reaches a hand toward the baby.

Miriam prays—not words, just anguished need slung heavenward—till she thinks her head and heart might burst.

The baby giggles.

The princess smiles.

Pharaoh's daughter reaches out bangled arms and draws Miriam's brother into her chest, hugging him close, nuzzling his soft hair with her chin, lifting him high into the air over the water so that even Miriam can see his smile and hear his happy squeal.

Hours later, Miriam stands on her own doorstep holding Moses in one arm, a sack of coins in the other—payment from Pharaoh's daughter, compensation for the wet nurse Miriam promised to find.

Mother opens the door. Whimpers.

Her expression leaps from fear to disbelief to ecstasy. She falls to her knees. Miriam rattles off the story, the bargain: care for the baby until he is weaned, old enough to return to the princess and be raised a prince of Egypt. Trembling, Mother takes her son, breathes him in, and rocks him there on the doorstep. She pulls Miriam down into a hug, sobbing, "Blessed, blessed girl," over and again into her hair. Miriam thinks her heart may fly away.

Throughout the day and into the night, family and friends flock to their house to smile on the miracle babe. A celebration breaks out, the likes of which no Hebrew has seen for years. With the party still going, the sound of Father's booming laughter filling their tiny home, Miriam sneaks away and crawls onto her pallet on the floor, dizzy with exhaustion, drunk with joy. Sleep is already tugging her down and under, lullaby waves, when she feels a calloused hand, gentle on her forehead. "Sweet Miriam, you have saved us all."

Miriam pushes up and throws her arms around Father's neck, breathing in his familiar scent, wood smoke and spices.

"Do you know what I think?" he says in a confidential whisper, brushing hair back from her face. "I think God will use our baby to save Israel. One day we will send him back to Pharaoh's household, and somehow, some way, God will use his position and learning to free us all. One day, thanks to you, we will no longer be slaves."

"Really?" Miriam sucks in air. "How long will we have to wait? How many years?"

Father taps a finger on her nose. "I don't know, darling, but when you have hope, time flies."

Miriam bounces up and down, no longer sleepy. "I can hardly wait."

I hate waiting.

If you haven't noticed, *wait* is a four-letter word. Coincidence? I think not.

It goes something like this:

God is good. Life is. . .pretty good. We have been following Jesus for a while, and many of our prayer requests—at least the most important ones—have been answered. Our faith is strong, the future brightly shining.

But then. . .we want something. Something that can't be bought, earned, or achieved. We have done our part—worked, grown, taken risks. Like young Miriam, we feel a promise ringing in our hearts—*Surely what I have prayed for will happen, and soon!*—but now we have reached the point where the decision is out of our hands, which means it is in God's. And at first that knowledge feels comforting. Our hopes, our heart, our happiness—all in the hands of God:

God the Father, who loves us and wants us to be happy.

God the omniscient, who knows us better than we know ourselves.

God the omnipotent, who has a plan and the power to execute it.

God the Creator, who controls the cosmos (surely this one little request will be easy for Him).

All He has to do is snap His all-powerful, all-loving fingers and. . .*done*. Wish granted. Prayer answered.

So we turn to God with our request, asking Him to do for us The Thing we cannot do for ourselves.

But there's a problem.

He doesn't do it.

He doesn't *not* do it, either.

He does nothing. (Nothing we can see, anyway.)

God doesn't say no, but neither does He say yes.

God says, "*Wait*."

Wait, what?

And here's the part that makes it really difficult to swallow: With God we don't get the kind of two-way human conversation we are used to. With prayer there's usually no verbal response from God, no explanation, no *"Here's My timeline for your life,"* no *"I hear you and I love you, but I can't give you what you want (yet) for the following loving, logical, and comforting reasons. . . ."* Instead, we pray and—nothing. Heaven resounds with His silence.

The longer the wait, the louder the silence.

But God is good, so we swallow hard and determine to wait patiently.

On good days, we turn back to prayer.

On bad days, we turn to social media. After two excruciating minutes—a contentment-shattering onslaught of clever stories, air-brushed images, and Big Exciting Announcements—we find our-selves sinking into the abyss: *Everyone else is happy. Everyone else is getting the thing I need, right on schedule.*

With knotted stomach and burning eyes, we try to regroup, drawing on life lessons we have collected over the years. Our earliest memories (thank you, Disney princesses) sing, "Believe in yourself! Follow your heart! Dreams come true!" Our middle and high school teachers' voices echo, "Never give up! You will get it soon because you are awesome (*everyone is awesome!*), and awesome people always suc-ceed!" Our Sunday school education encourages us, "Be the persistent widow!" Our adult theology reminds us, "Keep on asking, keep on knocking!"

So believe and dream and ask and knock and ask again and knock again we do. We turn to the Bible, to classic, sublimely comforting waiting passages like "Be strong and take heart and wait for the LORD" (Psalm 27:14), or this, the crown jewel of all the waiting passages:

> *Trust in the LORD and do good;*
>   *dwell in the land and enjoy safe pasture.*
> *Take delight in the LORD,*
>   *and he will give you the desires of your heart. . . .*
> *Be still before the LORD*
>   *and wait patiently for him.*
>
> PSALM 37:3–4, 7

With our faith renewed, we enjoy a little chuckle at our own expense, resign ourselves to wait patiently for a few more days (even weeks, if need be), and offer a prayer of apology for our impatience. In our contrition, we even do a heart check:

Dwelling in the land? *Check.*

Trusting in God? *Check.*

Delighting in the Lord? *Well, I could read and pray a little more, but. . .as of tomorrow. Check.*

And then we sit back and expect God to grant our request within the next seven to ten business days.

The problem is, we keep adding our own words to these waiting passages, and we have no idea we are doing it. We read them, we think we understand what they are saying, but we don't realize that subconsciously we keep tacking a little asterisked addendum onto the end of them that goes something like this:

> "Be strong and take heart and wait for the LORD. . ."*
> *because He is going to give you exactly what you want really, really soon.
> "Delight in the LORD, and he will give you the desires of your heart. . ."*
> *and that is a guaranteed formula: If you work hard and love God, then you will definitely, absolutely get your heart's desires—and "desires" includes all of your desires: admission and scholarships to the college you want; the job and salary you want; the guy and wedding you want; the apartment you want; the baby you want; the family you want; the friend you want; the health you want; the house you want; the happiness you want—as soon as you decide you want them. . .or pretty soon afterward.

And so, armed with our unintentionally asterisked waiting passages, we wait. We pray. We read more waiting passages. We pray some more. We try not to fidget. We delight in God. We delight in God some more. We humbly remind God that we are *delighting in Him* (teeth gritted, fists clenched, neck veins popping, but doggone it, *if we were any more delighted, we'd have a heart attack*). We alter our request to make it sound more spiritual, more like a prayer God would want to say yes to. We read more waiting passages. We get radical, and we fast. We ask friends to pray for us and fast with us.

Time passes. Too much time. More time than we'd ever imagined. As faith fades, doubts bloom. We question God, the Bible, ourselves.

The longer God's silence stretches, the more things start to break inside.

I don't know what you are waiting for right now, but we all are waiting for something. If you're like me, you're waiting on several somethings. Sometimes The Thing we seek is not even a thing, but a feeling: peace, joy, relief, release, security, home. For many of us, waiting seasons are the first time our faith has been truly tested. They present risk and opportunity in equal measure, making us ask the hard faith questions, making us fight to find—and accept—the answers.

Yes, No, Wait, and. . .Maybe

You have probably heard some preacher say, "When you ask God for something, He gives one of three answers: *Yes, no, or wait.*"

It's a good point, a nice sermon illustration. It makes sense.

But the problem is, *yes* is obvious. *Yes* means you get what you want. End of story, end of prayer request. Time to begin offering prayers of thanksgiving.

Yes is wonderful.

Yes is what we want every single time we ask God for something. *Yes* doesn't happen nearly as often, or as quickly, as we'd like.

And then there's *no*: Sometimes *no* is just *no*. You want to marry so-and-so, but he marries someone else. End of story. Find another guy.

But it's not always that clear-cut. The problem lies between the *no* and the *wait*. Because really, it's tough to tell the difference. Sometimes we think God's answer is *no*, but later—weeks, months, even decades later—the answer we thought was a *no* turns into a *yes*, so it turns out we actually had a *wait* all along.

And to make matters even more confusing, I believe God offers a fourth option—a theologically mind-bending option, which we will explore in greater depth in our chapter on persistence in prayer (chapter 6)—and it's this: *"Maybe. Ask Me again; you might talk Me into it."* And that answer may be the most maddening   but hope-sustaining—answer of all.

Mr. Letterman Jacket

But back to the quandary of the no-man's-land between *no* and *wait*. I have more examples of this from my own life than I can count.

When I was eighteen, I fell madly in love with the most heart-stoppingly handsome, sincerely spiritual, adorably sweet guy I had ever met, who also happened to be a quarterback on our college football team *and* my closest friend *and* my ride to church twice a week in his sporty little Dodge Avenger. I spent the first two years of my college career begging God to make this handsome, whole-package guy—we'll call him Mr. Letterman Jacket—fall in love with me.

Two miserably long years later, the summer after our sophomore year, a summer filled with lots of vague but promising vibes, God's answer felt imminent. The two of us were going to join some college friends for a weeklong Christian conference in Paris—Paris! The one in France! The romance capital of the world! And I was sure the time (and place) had come for God to answer my prayer. All summer I begged, "Please, Lord, make things clear by the time we go to Paris." So when the Love of My Life kept asking *every beautiful girl at the conference* out to dinner along the Champs-Élysées, I had no way of knowing if God's answer was the *non!* it appeared to be or if it was a *wait* disguised as a *no*.

I tormented myself with questions: If God's answer was indeed *no*, did that mean no just for dating Mr. Letterman Jacket right now, but wait for a boyfriend and marriage, because eventually God would say yes when the right non-idiot guy came along who saw me for the prize I was?

Or did it mean no to a boyfriend and marriage and a first kiss, and yes to a life of celibacy and single-serve microwavable meals to be enjoyed in the company of my library of books and my houseful of cats? (I'm not making fun of crazy cat ladies here. I *am* the crazy cat lady. I adore cats, books, and—foodies, hide your eyes—I have been known to enjoy many a microwaved meal.)

Confused? So was I. . .and it certainly wasn't the last time.

For many of us, waiting is unfamiliar terrain. New territory. We have forgotten how to navigate it—or maybe we never learned to begin with. And it's not entirely our fault. This world we live in is all about immediate gratification:

Fast food!

High-speed Internet!

Overnight shipping!

With speed as a cultural priority, it's no wonder *wait* feels like such a bad word. We don't believe in waiting.

Waiting is a waste of time.

Waiting is boring at best, agony at worst.

Waiting is the worst possible place to be.

A place? Yes, a place. Because waiting isn't just something we do; it's a place we live—usually against our will. It's a stage of life, a journey we take, a crucible for the heart.

The good news? We are not the first people to journey through the waiting wilderness. People in the Bible had to wait on God, and most were just as confused as we are, just as mystified and unhappy. Think for just a moment about some of these people, whose stories we will explore in the pages of this book:

Miriam, who may have expected God to use her baby brother to do something spectacular, but if you had told her how many years she would wait before seeing her hopes fulfilled, her people freed, I wonder how she would have felt, what would have happened to her faith. She spends decades—decades!—in slavery, waiting and wondering, before a burning bush finally lights a fire under Moses, and Miriam gets to dance out of Egypt, an aging woman leading her people in a song of praise.

David, who is anointed the future king of Israel when he is just a teenager, but spends years hiding in caves in the wilderness, fleeing his enemies, before claiming his promised throne.

Naomi, who loses her husband and two sons; devastated, she renames herself "Bitter" and goes home to wait for death to set her free. Yet God gives her a new family, a second chance.

Sarah, Hannah, Jacob, Ruth, Joseph, Mary, Gideon, Martha, Abraham—like us, they hoped; like us, they waited in the dark. They didn't know how their prayers, their dreams, their lives were going to turn out any more than you or I know our own futures. How easily we forget this when we read their stories!

Thanks to the Bible, we know their endings, the meanings of their stories, the things they could have done differently. But they simply lived their lives in the same way you and I do: not knowing the *ifs*, the *whens*, the *hows*, the *whys*. (Okay, sure, some of our Bible heroes did receive heavenly promises direct from God, but those promises rarely panned out in the way or in the timeline they expected, so I suggest we grant them a lot of grace, the kind of grace you and I would need in their same position.) Waiting was every bit as agonizing for them as it is for us. Every bit as confounding. Every bit as nail-biting.

As we explore their stories, they will equip us to live our own—particularly our problematic waiting times—with faith, patience, perspective, and a healthy dose of humor. Together we can plot a road map from scripture to help us navigate our own journeys through the barren waiting places.

The Road Ahead

I cannot pretend to foretell what lies ahead for you. I don't know how long you will wait—which prayers will be granted, which will be denied.

I can't promise you *yeses* for all of your prayers, but I can share with you the lessons I have prayed and studied and fought and resented and resisted and pleaded and fasted and pouted and wept and rejoiced and cajoled and wheedled and doubted and believed and laughed and hugged and sung and worshipped and persevered and kicked and screamed my way through.

I can offer you hope that the Bible can help you find the strength and spirituality you will need not just to *suffer through* your waiting times but to *grow through* them into the person God is shaping you to be. The person you might not even know you want to be.

I can offer you the insight that life *is* waiting—a series of waiting seasons between blessings, as God's plan for our lives unfolds one blind turn after the other. The insight that life *is* waiting—waiting for our dreams and desires, yes, but also waiting for heaven, where all that is lacking in this life and wrong with this world will be set right at last.

At this very moment, God is telling you, and me, and everyone we know—our families, our friends (even the picture-perfect airbrushed ones)—to wait for something. And we are all in for a challenging ride:

When God says, *"Wait,"* He doesn't tell us for how long.

When God says, *"Wait,"* we face one of life's greatest tests.

When God says, *"Wait,"* we have decisions to make.

When God says, *"Wait,"* we can control only two things: how we wait, and who we become along the way.

This book is about the journey of waiting, the space between answers, and the decisions we make while we live there.

So what are we waiting for? Let's get started.

Waiting Room Reading

For Further Study
You can read more about Miriam's life in Exodus 15:1–21 and Numbers 12.

Journal Prompt
Are you happy with how you are handling this season of waiting so far? Why or why not? What's the hardest part about waiting? Do you have questions about faith, God, or God's promises that you need to resolve?

Prayer Prompt
All my longings lie open before you, Lord;
my sighing is not hidden from you.
My heart pounds, my strength fails me;
even the light has gone from my eyes. . . .

Lord, I wait for you;
you will answer, Lord my God.
Psalm 38:9–10, 15

2
Pitfalls on Road Trips

Sarah's Story
The Day of Decision

Based on Genesis 16

*T*he sound of little-boy giggles rouses Sarah to a sleepy half consciousness. Eyes pressed closed against the morning light, she smiles and burrows deeper into her blankets. *I could listen to that sweet laugh forever*, she thinks, feeling a bubble of laughter rise in her own chest. *My son.* Her heart swells with affection.

The boy's giggles crescendo to happy shrieks, and through thin tent walls, Sarah hears little footsteps racing past. Heavier footfalls and a woman's singsong voice sound close behind, growing louder as someone else runs past Sarah's tent, chasing him. "Simeon, come back here, son!"

Sarah's eyes snap open. Reality and harsh late-morning light jar her to full wakefulness. Already the image of her son is fading, dissolving, shimmering like sun over heat-scorched sand. A mirage and nothing more. She stretches one shaky hand up, as if she could grasp the dream boy who visits her sleep—hold on to him, will him into existence. Burying her face in her pillow, she chokes back tears. It has been years since she has cried, decades since she has really believed she will hold the son Abraham has promised.

You should be past this by now, she tells herself as her chest tightens, spasms. *Seventy-five years old—can't you just accept the thing and die?*

She pushes up in bed on quivering arms, letting anger force her tears back down into the bitter box where she learned to store them years ago. *Never. I cannot—I will not—die childless.*

Swinging her legs out of the lumpy bed, pressing bare feet onto soft rugs, she stands up. Strong, her legs still feel strong. Strong enough to cradle a baby in her arms, to pace the floor for hours each night.

A baby. *Her* baby. The baby God promised Abraham all those years ago. Sarah barks a yelp of laughter even as her insides twist with resentment. The baby she *will* have now—before it is too late. Before her eyes grow too dull to savor his laughing brown eyes, her ears too dull to delight in his giggles, her arms too weak to rock him.

And in that moment, with another woman's son still squealing happily outside the tent walls, she makes up her mind: Today. She will do it today.

"Hagar!" she calls. "Hagar!"

Moments later, a small hand pushes open the thick flap; a dark head peeks inside, eyes lowered in subservience. "My lady?" Hagar says, raising dull brown eyes to meet Sarah's, a small, tentative smile on her thin lips.

Sarah scrutinizes her Egyptian maid for the thousandth time. Plain, so very plain—in looks and in personality. Obedient, humble, not one to question. Hagar will prove no real temptation for Abraham, no real competition for his eyes or his affections—just a simple young woman with the one thing Sarah lacks: a functional womb.

Hagar takes an uncertain step inside Sarah's room. "Shall I bring some breakfast, my lady? Or—?"

"No." Sarah tosses a shawl around her shoulders and raises herself to her full height. "Call Abraham. Tell him I must speak with him at once."

Confusion wrinkling her brow for a moment, Hagar inclines her head and bows out of the room.

As she leaves, Sarah runs fingers through her hair—still long and silky and dark as the night sky Abraham loves—and allows a surge of joy to drown out her objections, her doubt, her guilt. *I'm through with waiting. In ten months, I will hold my son.*

I know what it is to wait for a child. To allow hope to rise month after heartbreaking month, thinking, *Maybe this month, maybe this time. . . it just has to work this one time*; to imagine you feel every conceivable pregnancy symptom, from food aversions to breast pain—and then a pool of blood dashes your hopes again, sends you crashing into a chasm of darkness and despair you fear will never end. Let's drop in on some "highlights" from my baby-wait.

Mother's Day, Year One: Difficult, but Bearable

I grit my teeth and muscle my way through the church service, hands fisted at my sides, eyes trained on my Bible. I studiously avoid looking at all the happy mommies with their corsages and toddler-made bead necklaces. I am not reading the verses the preacher points us to about Mary the mother of Jesus and her journey through motherhood and faith; I am reading Psalm 119:82–84 (HCSB):

> *My eyes grow weary*
> *looking for what You have promised;*
> *I ask, "When will You comfort me?"*
> *Though I have become like a wineskin dried by smoke,*
> *I do not forget Your statutes.*
> *How many days must Your servant wait?*

Mother's Day, Year Two: A Battlefield, with Carnage

My preacher husband has insisted I go to the service in spite of my protests (not one of our best marital moments, I can tell you!). I'm there, but I'm angry. If looks could kill, all the glowing mommies in the room—my friends!—would be lasered to death by my envious glares. I'm not usually a jealous, malicious waiter, but today every ugly tendency I have ever faced roars to the surface. I am tempted by evil thoughts—nasty, spiteful, *Are you sure you're a Christian?* type thoughts. I wear a dress that flatters my nonpregnant figure and take secret comfort in the only "positive" thought I can find—that I'm not fighting post-baby muffin-top like everyone else my age. Yes, I'm thinking these things during church. No, I don't get struck by lightning. (Miracles happen. Grace abounds.)

I wish I could say I have handled my many waiting times with grace and elegance and faith, but I haven't. I'm sorry to say that, like Sarah, my patience, my faithful spirit, my plucky God-knows-what-He's-doing attitude tend to wilt the longer I have to wait for God's definitive answer.

But these (embarrassing) stories reveal some of the greatest pitfalls we face during our times of waiting. Waiting like this, for so long, does something to your hope, your heart. Whatever you are waiting for—true love or a baby, a job or a friend—the longer you wait, the more time God—and Satan—has to work on you.

My Waiting Friends

As I write these words, all of my friends are waiting for *something*.

One friend waits for The Plan. (A plan. Any plan.) She spent eight years building a fabulous résumé for a career she has just realized she hates. Now she wonders, *What in the world do I do with my life?*

Another friend waits for The Job. She has spent two years honing skills, buying suits, revising résumés; putting herself out there, daring to hope, getting so close. As confidence wanes, debt piles high.

Another friend has The Job but can't find The Guy. *Will I ever be loved? Will I always live alone?*

Another friend has The Guy, and *he* has The Job, but he is about to lose The Job, so they are about to move who knows where. *What happens next?*

Another friend has never had a true *best* friend. She has offered her heart, time and again, but never found her—*The* Friend, the Diana to her Anne, the Huck to her Tom—the one who can read her thoughts across the room, stay up laughing all night. She is happily married, close to her kids, but even so there's a hole in her heart, a lonely place.

Another friend waits to pursue The Dream. She accidentally got pregnant in her first year of marriage and decided to postpone grad school and career plans. Now, as much as she enjoys motherhood and adores her babies, she worries, *Have I missed my chance?*

Meanwhile, another friend lives The Dream—great guy, cool job, fun town, cute dog—but can't have The Baby. She is young, she is healthy, and she has "unexplained infertility." One by one her friends become mothers without her. Every twenty-eight days she bleeds to death.

Another friend waits for The Cure. She has seen a dozen doctors, tried every traditional and homeopathic solution she can find. Spent thousands of dollars. Still she suffers; still she waits.

Another friend waits for The Return: Her son has strayed from God. He is a good kid—respectful, trustworthy, talented—but God is low on his priority list.

Several friends wait for The Escape: the day beloved husbands fully break free from chains of pornography and substance abuse.

Another friend waits for The Miracle. She rests in a hospital bed, hoping her body will hold the baby she so desperately wants. She has lost this battle before, and now the doctors aren't making any guarantees. All she can do is rest and wait and pray. *Please. . .*

All of these are real situations going on *right now* in my circle of friends. Real women, real pain. Friends I pray for and cry with. Many live within a few miles of my house; some live far away.

Waiting comes in myriad forms, but we all face it. Every woman everywhere. Some waits are the soul-killing, life-threatening kind; other waits are lighter, affecting our happiness and daily comfort. Outside the blessed life my friends and I lead here in the first world, women around the world wait for desperate things, life-or-death things. This very minute, thousands of Syrian refugees wait to escape danger, many with small children in tow. They wait in terror, every step a risk. Remembering their kind of waiting puts my own problems in perspective and makes me grateful for all I have even now, the countless daily gifts—freedom, food, housing—that I have never had to wait for.

No matter what kind of wait you are enduring today, be it the soul-killing kind of wait or the daily-joy-stealing kind of wait, hear this, know this: your pain, your doubt, your struggles, your feelings are real. Valid. You have a wound that needs tending. Even small cuts can turn septic and poison the whole body. In this book we will address waiting of all scopes and scales.

The Pitfalls of Waiting

Sarah waited longer than most of us have even been alive. In a sense, her life is a study in waiting. God has promised Abraham and Sarah a child, but He left out one tiny detail: *when* (Genesis 15:1–6).

Decades pass.

Faith fades.

Sarah falters.

Convinced that God's promise isn't happening, Sarah decides to take matters into her own hands before it's too late. (Because, let's be honest: she blew past *too late* thirty-five years ago.) I feel Sarah's pain. I understand how she got there.

I have often thought to myself, *The worst part of waiting is the not knowing. I wish God would just give me a yes or no so I can move on with life.*

Have you ever thought something like this:

If I knew I wasn't going to find true love, maybe I could get busy building a fulfilling life as a single woman.

If I knew I wasn't going to have the career I've longed for, maybe I could devote my time and energy to other things.

If I knew I wasn't going to get pregnant, maybe I could find a way to accept it and move forward, consider other options.

I tell myself my problem is just *not knowing.* Dealing with uncertainty. I tell myself I wouldn't mind waiting so much if God just told me, *"Yes, you're going to get what you want, but buckle up for a long ride—it's going to take a while."* I convince myself I could handle that kind of wait.

But who am I kidding? Sarah got the *if*—the promise direct from God, the money-back guarantee—and still she struggled. She wanted more. She wanted *when.*

I want more, too.

When I'm waiting, I want more than just a *yes* or *no* from God. It's not enough to know *if*; I want to know *when*. I want a timeline. A fat red circle on the calendar. Like Job, I pray:

> *If only You would appoint a time for me*
> *and then remember me. . . .*
> *If so, I would wait all the days of my struggle*
> *until my relief comes.*
> *You would call, and I would answer You.*
>
> JOB 14:13–15 HCSB

I'm going to wait two years and nine months before I get pregnant, you say? Okeydokey. I don't love that timeline, but I can work with it. I'll write two novels and take a few awesome kid-free vacations and sleep late while I can, and see a ton of movies. I'll do the Pinterest thing and make a cute countdown calendar, and I'll find a way to be happy the whole time I'm waiting.

But life doesn't work that way; God doesn't work that way. It is in the *not knowing* that God can work on our heart, our faith, our character. It is in the *not knowing* that 2 Peter 1 and James 1 collide:

> *For this very reason, make every effort to add to your*
> *faith goodness; and to goodness, knowledge; and to*
> *knowledge, self-control; and to self-control, persever-*
> *ance; and to perseverance, godliness; and to godliness,*
> *mutual affection; and to mutual affection, love. For if*
> *you possess these qualities in increasing measure, they*
> *will keep you from being ineffective and unproductive*
> *in your knowledge of our Lord Jesus Christ.*
>
> 2 PETER 1:5–8

Christians are meant to grow—to become godlier, more loving, more self-controlled, better at persevering—so we don't stagnate spiritually. Spiritual growth doesn't happen automatically, accidentally, or overnight. Spiritual growth is a lifetime process we never outgrow. It takes conscious effort—*every* effort, in fact. The perfectionist in me finds this both overwhelming and comforting—overwhelming because I want to be done growing (meaning *perfect*) yesterday; comforting because I realize I'm not supposed to be done growing yet. Character is built slowly: step-by-step, choice by choice, even mistake by mistake, one strength building on another over time. Smack in the middle of this character-building process we find the trait we desperately need when we are waiting: perseverance. Now let's pair this passage with what James says about perseverance:

> *Consider it pure joy, my brothers and sisters, whenever you face trials of many kinds, because you know that the testing of your faith produces perseverance. Let perseverance finish its work so that you may be mature and complete, not lacking anything.*
>
> JAMES 1:2–4

We will work up to the "pure joy" part later (because this is only chapter 2, and we don't want anyone's brain exploding), but for now, did you catch that last phrase—"*let* perseverance finish its work"—as in it's up to us to allow that work to happen so we can grow? As in trials produce perseverance, and perseverance can lead to spiritual maturity, but we have to *let it happen*, not fight the process? (I know, probably not what you wanted to hear—me neither.) *If we let Him*, God can use our waiting journeys to shape us, to make us into the people He created us to be.

Knowing our weakness, knowing our need, God offers us many stories of godly people who have wrestled with waiting with varying success. People like Sarah, who received a definitive promise from God but then crumbled in the face of bleak fact: seventy-five-year-old women just don't have babies. The good news for those of us (all of us) who wait imperfectly? Many of our fellow waiters in the Bible got second chances. And third and fourth and fifth, and on and on goes the grace of God.

Waiting seasons aren't fun, but they are opportunities. Through our waiting seasons—yes, through the not knowing—we can build character one step at a time. Through our waiting seasons, perseverance can gradually "finish" its never-ending work in us. As waiting does its thing, and God does His, we get the chance to become our best selves, the people God designed us to be.

Pitfalls on Waiting Journeys

The temptation, during waiting times, is to torment ourselves with questions we can't answer, questions *no one* can answer: *Why? Why me? How long?*

In the chapters that follow, we are going to focus on the questions we *can* answer: *How will I wait?* and *Who will I become along the way?*

Choosing who we want to be during waiting seasons starts with identifying the Enemy's traps so we can avoid them. The pitfalls of waiting are many, but here I'll list some of the most dangerous, along with some thoughts that accompany them. Perhaps these thoughts will sound familiar:

The pitfall of bitterness:
I can't believe this has happened to me. I don't deserve this. I've spent years trusting and serving God, and this *is what I get in return?*

The pitfall of selfishness:
I can't be there for anyone else—it's all I can do just to get through each day. I have to look out for myself right now.

The pitfall of self-reliance:
God is not taking care of me, so I'll have to take care of myself.

The pitfall of doubt:
Does God love me? Does He even know I exist? Because there's no way the compassionate heavenly Father I grew up believing in would let a

beloved daughter go through something like this—so either He doesn't hear, doesn't care, or doesn't exist.

The pitfall of manipulation:
I can't stand it anymore. If God won't fix my problems, then I will. My plan may not be exactly biblical, but I can't sit around and wait forever. I have to do something about this.

The pitfall of cynicism:
Just look at that happy woman over there—she had better enjoy happiness while it lasts. She has no idea how life can turn on a dime.

The pitfall of envy:
Why would God give her the thing I've been begging for all these months when she didn't even really want it? She will never appreciate it the way I would. She doesn't deserve it.

The pitfall of self-pity:
Everyone else is happy but me. Everyone else has what she wants except me. No one cares. No one understands. I'm so alone.

The pitfall of faithlessness:
God has forgotten me. His promises are failing. I don't think they're ever coming true. I don't know why I even bother praying.

The pitfall of depression:
My life is over. I'll never be happy again unless this waiting ends.

At some point in my times of waiting, I have indulged in every one of these thoughts. Sometimes I have fallen all the way down the rabbit hole (ahem, Mother's Day, Year Two) and had to find a way to scramble back out. Ephesians 6 teaches us to put on the armor of God. When we go into spiritual battle, we will need to know where we require special protection—which parts of our spiritual armor have vulnerabilities or even gaping holes. Satan loves to take advantage of our weaknesses, but

God can turn even weakness into strength (Hebrews 11:34).

We won't explore every pitfall at length in this chapter—we will address them at different points throughout the book—but Sarah's story helps us see some of the dangerous places these pitfalls can lead to if left unchecked.

God Gets (and Gives) the Last Laugh

In Genesis 12 (eleven years before the Hagar Incident), God tells Abraham and Sarah to leave their family, their home, and go. . .somewhere. Final destination TBA. Can you imagine packing up and moving without knowing where you are going, no address to plug into the GPS?

So not only does Sarah spend fifty or sixty years struggling with infertility, but she also leaves the place she knows, the people she loves, to join her husband on an endless road trip, occasionally being sort of kidnapped by foreign rulers because she is so gorgeous (Genesis 12:10–20; 20)—not what you'd call an easy life. As Sarah's baby-wait stretches long, she succumbs to bitterness, doubt, faithlessness, and manipulation. When we consider the big picture of Sarah's life, it's easier to understand how she got to the desperate place, the "Hey, Abraham, I've got a great idea—have a baby with my servant girl!" place.

The Hagar Incident brings trouble and heartache on everyone involved (Genesis 16). Even though God steps in to prevent absolute disaster, some long-term conflict remains. When we try to take over and do things our way instead of God's way, we may face some painful consequences.

But do you know what I adore about God? He doesn't define Sarah by this moment of weakness. Does Sarah forever grapple with the irreversible consequences of that unfortunate decision? Yes. Does it affect her entire family, including her son Isaac, the child of promise God eventually gives? Yes. But even so, God doesn't permanently label Sarah "the crazy infertile lady who blew it and ruined everybody's lives." Notice God's positive words about Sarah, seventeen hundred years later, in the Bible's first century writings: "By faith even Sarah, who was past childbearing age, was enabled to bear children because she considered him faithful who had made the promise" (Hebrews 11:11).

And 1 Peter 3:6 commends Sarah, encouraging us to imitate her fearlessness and loyalty to her husband: we are Sarah's daughters "if [we] do what is right and do not give way to fear."

Even though Sarah messed up—lost faith, *broke* faith, took over—she still got the blessing she sought. God didn't unmake His promise. Sarah ends her life blessed and laughing. *Laughing!* Laughing at herself, laughing with friends, laughing with God.

One year before Sarah's miracle baby is born, this funny scene, recorded in Genesis 18:1–15, plays out: Three visitors show up at Abraham's tent to deliver a message from God. According to the cultural customs of the day, Sarah and the servants make dinner for the men then leave them to it. According to the cultural customs of *everyone's* day, Sarah hides in the entrance to the tent behind them, eavesdropping. (What other choice did she have when her husband couldn't text her updates from under the table?)

To paraphrase the conversation, it goes something like this:

Abraham: Thank you, friends, for joining us for dinner. As you may have heard, my wife recently celebrated her eighty-ninth birthday, and—well, there's still no word on that baby God promised. (*Wiggles bushy eyebrows—hint, hint, hint.*) Do you gentlemen have any updates from The Man Upstairs?

Messenger: Actually, yes. We will return about this time next year, and Sarah will have a son.

Sarah (*peeking out through the tent opening*): (*She gasps in surprise, then tries to picture her own bent body swollen with child and Abraham's clumsy fingers struggling to swaddle an infant. She presses hands hard against her mouth, trapping giggles inside.*) Seriously? After all these years—me wrinkled, Abraham worn out—*now* I get this blessing? (*A snicker escapes.*)

Messenger to Abraham (*cocking one eyebrow*): Why is your wife laughing?

Abraham (*cheeks growing red behind his gray beard*): My wife? I, uh, she, er. . .

Messenger: Is anything too hard for the Lord? I *will* return this time next year, and she *will* have a son.

Abraham (*holding up a finger*): Excuse me for a moment, gentlemen. (*He hurries into the tent and corners Sarah, who is busy arranging pillows on the bed, whistling to herself with her innocent face on. Abraham shakes an arthritic finger at her.*) Stop doing that!

Sarah: Doing what? The pillows need—

Abraham: Stop laughing at God! Do you want to blow our chance?

Sarah (*still working the wide-eyed innocent face*): Hmm? What laughing? I wasn't laughing. I don't even know what laughing is.

Abraham: (*He gives her the* Don't mess with me; I know what you're thinking *look he has spent their whole marriage perfecting.*)

Sarah: (*She gives him the* No, you don't know what I'm thinking *look she also has spent their whole marriage perfecting.*) Must have been that new servant girl—you know what a giggler she is.

Abraham (*rolling his eyes, fighting a grin*): (*He turns and stalks out of the tent. Just before it closes behind him, he pops his gray head back in.*) Yes, you did laugh!

Sarah: Humph.

(*The tent snaps shut. Sarah chuckles some more.*)

A year later, in one of my favorite biblical scenes ever, Sarah nuzzles the newborn son she never thought she would hold, sharing a laugh with God. She even names her son Isaac—*"He Laughs"*—not only in honor of the joy God has brought to her life—a joy so great it bubbles over into endless laughter, all the laughter she missed all those long years—but also in memory of her own faithless laughter, her moment of doubt. From now on, every time she calls her son's name, she will remember, *Once I laughed at God, but now God laughs with me. Now He shares my joy.*

Sarah wrestled with, and fell prey to, many—if not all—of the temptations you and I face during our waiting seasons. She fell, and fell hard. She wept, and wept hard.

But that was not the end of her story. Her faith survived, her marriage survived, her laughter survived. I don't know how your waiting story ends—how long will you wait, and will God say yes?—but this I know: you may be sad and struggling now, but God can restore laughter in the end.

He can bring back joy after months, years, even decades of waiting.

He can bring back joy after you have doubted and questioned.

He can bring back joy after you have made mistakes—yes, even the kind with lasting consequences.

He can use your wait to shape you, make you stronger and more Christlike.

Waiting is a journey of testing, fraught with spiritual danger but rife with opportunity. Like Sarah, like us, each of our Bible heroes had to decide how to think and who to be during their in-between times. They didn't get everything they wanted, but many of them became the people *God* wanted them to be. God used their waiting times to shape them into instruments He could use for powerful purposes.

If you have already given in to some of waiting's pitfalls, if you are struggling even now as you read, hear this, know this: Your story isn't over. You can stumble and fall, you can question and doubt—and God can help you set it right. You can get the last laugh. Best of all, you can laugh *with God*.

Waiting Room Reading

For Further Study
For Sarah's full life story, read Genesis 11:27–23:20.

Journal Prompt
Take some time to identify which specific pitfalls are most threatening to you. What scriptures can help you battle those temptations? Here are a few that have helped me: *bitterness*: James 5:7–11; *doubt*:

Psalm 37:25–26, James 5:16–18; *manipulation*: Psalm 33:11–22, 2 Peter 3:13–15; *cynicism*: Psalm 40:1–3 (I love *The Message* version of this one!); *envy*: Psalm 73, James 3:13–18.

Prayer Prompt

I remain confident of this:
* I will see the goodness of the LORD*
* in the land of the living.*
Wait for the LORD;
* be strong and take heart*
* and wait for the LORD.*

PSALM 27:13–14

3
Survival Skills for Spiritual Waiting

Hannah's Story
Year after Year

Based on 1 Samuel 1

Trip to Shiloh, Year One

Hannah snuggles in bed with Elkanah after the sacrifice, their noses almost touching. "What did you pray for at the temple today?" she asks, tracing his stubbled jawline with one finger, still learning its shape.

"For you." He brushes a soft kiss against her forehead. "For our life to come. For strong sons with big appetites, sweet daughters with their mother's eyes," he teases, pressing a warm palm against her flat stomach.

She giggles, a series of images dancing across her imagination: a dark-eyed girl with dimples and braids; a fat baby boy, his legs a series of chubby rolls.

"Isaac," she says. "We'll name the first boy Isaac, because he will make us laugh. But for now. . .I'm happy just to be here with you."

Trip to Shiloh, Year Four

Elkanah wraps a strong arm around Hannah. She curves her back into his chest, hoping he doesn't realize she is using the position to hide tears.

"What did you pray for at the temple today?" She forces her voice steady.

"For us," he says, his breath warm against her ear. "It will happen soon—I believe that." His strong voice radiates confidence, confidence she wishes she could feel. She tries to borrow it, but the harder she chases, the faster it flees. He squeezes her tight. "Next year you'll bring a baby here with you."

She nods, not trusting her voice. Hoping he accepts the nod, doesn't ask questions, make her speak, find out how much she has begun to doubt.

Trip to Shiloh, Year Nine

Hannah curls alone in bed, feeling the cold from Elkanah's empty spot seep over to her side. She presses fingertips against her eyelids so hard they set bursts of starlight swirling. How she wishes bright spots could erase today's images: Peninnah, Elkanah's other wife, the center of every conversation around the well. All the women passing six-month-old Jacob around, marveling that Peninnah is already expecting again, her fourth child in as many years. *God has smiled upon you, Peninnah. Elkanah can't get enough of you, can he? Every time he looks at you, you get pregnant!* Hannah fights to unremember their sideways glances, the accusations hurled without words: *What sin did Hannah commit that she can't get pregnant, while Peninnah can't stop?*

It is midnight before Elkanah creeps in, his every movement an apology. "Sorry," he whispers. "Peninnah needed me. She's sick again, and the baby won't sleep."

"I don't want to know," Hannah snaps. "If she needs you so much, why don't you stay with her tonight?"

Elkanah's silence cuts worse than anger.

Regret spears her. "I'm sorry." She reaches a hand out blind, wanting to take back the words, draw him in close. "I'm glad you came to me." She can't find his hand in the dark.

Trip to Shiloh, Year Twelve

Hannah sits beside Elkanah at the feast, embarrassed by the double portion of meat on her plate, pushing it around, choking down small bites for Elkanah's sake. Peninnah's resentful gaze scalds her, even across the long table. Elkanah leans in close, whispering, "You're all I want, all I need. Aren't I worth more than ten sons?" The tears surprise her. *After so many years, you should be beyond sorrow.* She blinks hard.

Halfway through the meal, Peninnah's two-year-old, Joshua, toddles over and tugs on Hannah's skirts. Hannah can't help but adore him; she cared for him herself all those long months when Peninnah huddled in bed, listless and crying. Sometimes he still gets confused, calls both women Mama. Joshua raises his arms with an impish smile, purple leaves clutched in one pudgy fist. For half a breath she can't help the fantasy: *What if he were mine?* She draws him into her lap, squeezing the squishy skin at his waist. He squirms sideways, squealing, and pushes the flowers into her chest.

She plucks the crumpled offering from his fingers. "For me?" He nods proudly, and she nestles her chin into his soft, dark hair. "From you?"

Giggling, he shakes his head no. "From Mama. *Real* Mama."

Hannah's stomach coils into a fist, and she looks more closely at the blooms. Mandrakes. The flower of fertility, or so all the old women said. Eat their fruit, inhale their heady scent, hang them over your bed, and you will be pregnant in no time. If she had a coin for every time she had heard that, tried that. . .

Humiliation sets fire to her cheeks. Joshua slips from her lap, toddles back to his mother. *Real Mama.* Across the table, Peninnah picks him up, flashing a grin at Hannah, her smile a sword. "For you," she mouths. "For tonight." Around the table, other women are watching, weighing, whispering.

Hannah staggers to her feet. She feels Elkanah's fingers brush against her wrist—*Stay*—but she is already gone.

Tear-blind, she stumbles outside, gasping. Hearing Elkanah's voice calling—so small, so far, he has never been so far away—she lifts her skirts and breaks into a sprint, not knowing where she is headed, just running. Somewhere. Anywhere. Away.

She doesn't remember getting there, doesn't remember heaving open the heavy door, but she is in the temple, violent sobs ripping her apart, shredding her heart, turning her insides out. Eyes squeezed shut, tears raining down. Fists clenched tight, nails drawing blood. Gasping with grief, clawing at prayer.

She can't make a sound, can hardly draw breath. For a moment, she wishes the sorrow would do it—kill her. End this. How can a heart, so long dead, keep on beating?

Somehow her mind forms words.

Remember me, Lord. Remember me. Give me a son, and I will give him back to You.

A raspy voice breaks in: "Enough! Enough of your wine! For shame, coming drunk to God's temple!"

Horrified, Hannah's eyes fly open. She swipes at her swollen eyes and finds the priest Eli glaring at her from his chair by the temple door. His eyes deliver the wrath of God. She chokes out words, her chest hitching with sobs. "Not. . .so. . .my lord! I pour. . .pour out my soul. . .to the Lord. . .from grief."

Eli strokes his long beard, studying her. He gives a tiny nod, waves her forward. He takes her trembling hands in his, turns over the palms, brushes calloused thumbs over the crescent-shaped wounds in her palms. His eyes soften, crinkle up at her. "Go in peace, daughter. May God grant what you have asked." He closes his eyes and mouths a prayer of his own.

Hannah's breath stops. Hope, long banished, sprouts wings in her chest: shy, cautious, the tiniest of flutterings. "Thank you, my lord," she breathes.

That night she reaches for Elkanah, kissing words into his shoulder. "I prayed in the temple today." He wakes; she smiles; hope flies in the dark.

This went on year after year (1 Samuel 1:7).

Not day after day, week after week, or even month after month, but *year after year*.

Some of us can barely wait for our coffee to brew in the morning without a nervous breakdown (don't judge me); how in the name of all that is good and holy are we supposed to survive weeks, months, or years of delay for the *real* blessings?

When first we begin to wait, we may be okay for a while. We

drift along, treading water, sure our circumstances will change any day now.

Any.

Day.

Now.

But when things don't change, and the wait stretches longer than we were prepared for (and let's be honest: *any* delay is longer than we were prepared for), we may begin to flounder spiritually. The spiritual habits we have had, the prayer life we have led, the simple, unexamined faith we have relied on—they aren't enough anymore. If we don't seriously up our efforts at survival, we start to tire, to struggle, to drown.

Is that where you are now? Legs cramping, lungs protesting, arms aching, struggling to keep your head above water, choking on mouthfuls of salt water?

During seasons of waiting, we have to develop a new set of spiritual survival skills. We have to build new muscles, try different strategies, expand our approach. We might have to find a life preserver to help us stay afloat, or climb up into a life raft. What are these survival skills for spiritual waiting, and how do we develop them?

Survival Skill Number One: Show Up to Prayer

Hannah was a woman of prayer. When first we meet her in 1 Samuel 1, we find her trying to eat at the house of the Lord. But her bitter rival wife has provoked her—dug a knife into the painful wound and twisted—to the point of despair. Hannah can't eat, can't even stay in the same room. How tempting it must have been to respond in an unrighteous way. Maybe Hannah was a fighter and she was tempted to stand there and throw down with Peninnah—duke it out once and for all. (Horrible confession that reveals how un-Jesus-like I can be: I kind of wish the Bible gave us a scene where Hannah goes Jackie Chan on Peninnah.) Or maybe Hannah was a runner, tempted to go hide and throw herself an epic pity party (totally what I would have done), but Hannah decided to be a pray-er:

Once when they had finished eating and drinking in Shiloh, Hannah stood up. Now Eli the priest was sitting on his chair by the doorpost of the LORD's house. In her deep anguish Hannah prayed to the LORD, weeping bitterly. . . .

As she kept on praying to the LORD, Eli observed her mouth. Hannah was praying in her heart, and her lips were moving but her voice was not heard. Eli thought she was drunk and said to her, "How long are you going to stay drunk? Put away your wine."

"Not so, my lord," Hannah replied, "I am a woman who is deeply troubled. I have not been drinking wine or beer; I was pouring out my soul to the LORD. Do not take your servant for a wicked woman; I have been praying here out of my great anguish and grief."

Eli answered, "Go in peace, and may the God of Israel grant you what you have asked of him."

1 SAMUEL 1:9–10, 12–17

Even after so many years of begging for the same thing, so many years with arms still empty, Hannah kept praying. And hers were no wooden, distant, *Why do I waste my time?* prayers. No, she humbly poured out her soul to God. Even after all those years. Year after year.

Think about it: Prayer is what caught Eli's attention. Prayer secured the promise Hannah needed. Prayer paved the way for her to have a son—her miracle baby, Samuel.

When you have been waiting forever, you will be tempted to stop praying.

Pray anyway.

You might think, *I've already asked God for this five gazillion times. He must be sick of hearing from me.*

Pray anyway.

You might think, *I have nothing new to say.*

Pray anyway.

You might have to get creative to feel connected—take prayer walks, sit outside, find a prayer partner, write down your prayers—but don't give up on prayer during this time. You need it now more than ever.

(For a more thorough look at prayer, see chapters 5 and 6.)

Survival Skill Number Two: Show Up to Worship

I wonder if Hannah gradually came to dread the family's annual trek to Shiloh to worship. As with all family traditions, this one probably came to serve as a marker for the progress of their family life: "Remember the year Peninnah was pregnant (again) and the caravan had to stop every five minutes so she could throw up?" "Remember the year Hannah had a miscarriage on the way?" "Remember the year all Peninnah's kids got a stomach bug on the last night?"

As years passed, the experience must have darkened. With competition intensifying between wives, Elkanah fought harder to make Hannah feel special, but his kindness only fueled the feud. How Hannah's memories must have been colored with loss, shot through with grief, warped by unkindness. Happy memories for others, all pain for Hannah.

Year after year.

I wonder if Hannah ever thought about skipping worship altogether, staying home alone with her grief.

In year two of my struggle to get pregnant, six women in our small congregation got pregnant, all due within three weeks of each other. Six women, three weeks, one church. (I know, it's ridiculous. Please take a moment to feel very, very sorry for me.) How excited the whole church was, especially when they announced that all six babies would be boys. I could hardly walk through the fellowship without brushing up against someone's burgeoning belly—or worse, a whole group of bellies circled together as the Mom-to-Be Club rubbed tummies, felt babies kick, compared notes on birth plans and breastfeeding, giggling and glowing and just looking so doggone happy. (To their credit, they weren't being insensitive or unkind, or trying to leave me out; it was just one of those things: they couldn't help being pregnant all together, and I couldn't help being infertile all alone.) It was all I could do not to gnash my teeth and wail through every church service.

But you know what? I kept showing up to church. I hid in the bathroom and cried sometimes, and I made a lot of emergency Starbucks mocha consolation runs on the way home, but I kept showing up. Why? Because my husband was the campus minister and I didn't want him to get fired. No, that's not really why. (Okay, maybe sometimes it was a little bit why.) But really, during that desert period, I needed worship more than ever. I needed time with God's people (even the pregnant ones) to restore my faith and rekindle my connection with the Lord. I needed to pray, to sing, to hear the spoken Word, to be around people who could lift my faith when it flagged. I needed to *serve* in the church, to get my eyes off my own sadness.

It was worship that brought Hannah the blessing she sought.

When you are waiting, you will have despairing days. Days when you want to hole up in your room and huddle in the dark with sad thoughts. Worshipping God, especially in a congregational setting, will feel like the worst idea in the world. How can joyful songs come from a heart riddled with loss?

Don't give in.

Worship will minister to you in ways you don't even know you need. It will fill holes in your soul you don't realize you have, gaps you can't fill yourself.

Worship might make you feel vulnerable and exposed. It might tug on emotional chords you would rather keep hidden, protected and private. It might make you "go there" when you would really rather not. It might make you cry at church—maybe even ugly cry, just like Hannah—but you know what? *That's not a bad thing.* God wants to meet us on an emotional level, and worship is one of the ways He draws us out and connects with us. Worship proves especially powerful in times when God feels distant and our prayer life feels blocked.

Sometimes worship corrects our thinking. There's something about singing—not just singing along in a car, but standing beside other Christians, singing to live music—that wakes something inside and even helps us make sense of biblical truths. I love the psalmist's confession in Psalm 73. He has been looking around, envying godless people because their lives seem so carefree, so easy. He is caught in a spiral of bitter, godless, envious thoughts—until he steps into the house of God to worship:

> *But as for me, my feet had almost slipped;*
> *I had nearly lost my foothold.*
> *For I envied the arrogant*
> *when I saw the prosperity of the wicked. . . .*
> *When I tried to understand all this,*
> *it troubled me deeply*
> *till I entered the sanctuary of God;*
> *then I understood their final destiny.*
> PSALM 73:2–3, 16–17

Worship gives us perspective, reminding us that as big as our problems feel, as much as we hurt, there's a whole world out there in need of God. In need of *our faith* to make a difference.

Worship reminds us of the power of God—the power He can exercise on our behalf.

Worship reminds us that God is God and we are not.

Worship helps us understand and accept God's love.

Worship helps us appeal to God even when we don't know how to pray.

Worship helps us heal.

Worship helps us wait.

Survival Skill Number Three: Show Up for Time in God's Word

Waiting can bleed us dry—drain our hope, our happiness, our heart. But God's Word can fill us back up again. If waiting is a desert, then God's Word is the oasis where we pause to refresh our water supply.

When I'm waiting on God, prayer takes more energy and work than usual. But the Bible has been my saving grace. When God seems silent on the other end of my prayers, His Word is the cord that keeps us connected and helps me find His voice. When my path weaves down into the darkness of "the valley of the shadow of death" (Psalm 23:4 KJV), the Bible is a "lamp for my feet, a light on my path" (Psalm 119:105).

- During times of loneliness and financial strain, I have loved these words from God to Moses:

  "I have indeed seen the misery of my people in Egypt.
  I have heard them crying out. . .and I am concerned
  about their suffering."

  EXODUS 3:7

What does this scripture show us? "I have *seen*. . .I have *heard*. . .I *am concerned*." God sees, God hears, God cares.

Repeat that to yourself a thousand times a day if need be:
God sees.
God hears.
God cares.

- When I was waiting to find The Guy, I took great comfort in passages where God declares His love for us:

  "Since you are precious and honored in my sight,
      and because I love you,
  I will give people in exchange for you,
      nations in exchange for your life."

  ISAIAH 43:4

"Therefore I am now going to allure her;
  I will lead her into the wilderness
  and speak tenderly to her. . . .
"In that day," declares the LORD,
  "you will call me 'my husband'. . . .
I will betroth you to me forever."

HOSEA 2:14, 16, 19

- As our baby-waiting days stretched long, Satan kept whispering, "God doesn't love you; He wants you to suffer." I began to question God's kindness. But then I found this:

Yet this I call to mind
  and therefore I have hope:
Because of the LORD's great love we are not consumed,
  for his compassions never fail.
They are new every morning;
  great is your faithfulness.
I say to myself, "The LORD is my portion;
  therefore I will wait for him."
The LORD is good to those whose hope is in him,
  to the one who seeks him;
it is good to wait quietly for the salvation of the LORD. . . .
Though he brings grief, he will show compassion,
  so great is his unfailing love.
For he does not willingly bring affliction
  or grief to anyone.

LAMENTATIONS 3:21–26, 32–33

What a comfort to realize that God doesn't want us to be miserable. When difficulty comes, He hurts with us. Just as a parent suffers when a child goes through a painful time of growth, so God suffers with us, His children.

- When we miscarried in the same week that we moved out of our dream home and moved two states away from family and friends, I thought I'd wait forever for God to heal us and restore happiness. For months I clung to Psalm 86:

Bring joy to your servant, Lord,
   for I put my trust in you. . . .
Teach me your way, LORD,
   that I may rely on your faithfulness;
give me an undivided heart,
   that I may fear your name. . . .
Give me a sign of your goodness,
   that my enemies may see it and be put to shame,
   for you, LORD, have helped me and comforted me.
                                   VERSES 4, 11, 17

Even now I return to these passages whenever my faith grows weary, and their effect on me is almost instantaneous. By helping to lift my eyes off problems and up to heaven, they restore my faith, revive my hope, and remind me of God's love.

I urge you to find scriptures like these—*your* scriptures—to plot your course through in-between times. Find the passages that fix you, that save you, while you wait. Let them serve as your road map through the lonely, unmarked waiting territory. Carry them with you. Write them on your fridge, your mirror, your hand, your heart. Read them over and over until you believe them and their message sinks deep down into your soul and changes you—even heals you.

When Amber broke up with the boy she had hoped to marry, she watched friend after friend fall in love, experience epic romance, get engaged and married. As her friends drove around town listening to sappy love songs and picking out reception playlists, Amber drove alone, blasting "You Give Love a Bad Name" as loud as her ears could take it. The year after the breakup—the year she thought she would be planning her own wedding—she was a bridesmaid three times, and that was just the beginning. Amber survived by printing and laminating three scriptures about envy. She kept them in her wallet and read them anytime she was tempted with envy (which for a while was every 7.3 minutes). That little laminated lifesaver salvaged her sanity and her relationships on more than one occasion, most notably this one:

For the twentieth time, Amber finds herself at a bridal shower for a younger friend. A friend she adores but is tempted to resent. *It's not fair, God! Why does she get to get married, fresh out of college, and here I sit, going on mercy dates with dorky guys?* When the friend opens the third set of white dishes, to a chorus of *ooh*s and *aah*s, Amber can't fake-smile anymore. She sneaks out and hides herself in the room with the coats and purses, sobbing on the floor. With shaking hands, she pulls out her laminated scriptures and reads them through tears, over and over and over. In the mysterious way of God, the scriptures go to work reminding her of what's true. Amber's sobs fade. Her heart softens. She finds she can pray, can release her pain to God. She finds she doesn't hate her friend after all. She finds strength to dry her eyes, take a deep breath, and return to the shower. It feels like days, but it's only been ten minutes. She finds she can clap, even throw in an *ooh* or *aah* of her own, and genuinely share in her friend's happiness.

That's the power of the Word of God.

Survival Skill Number Four: Show Up for Fun

Sometimes when we are waiting for the life we want, we forget to enjoy the life we already have. It may be incomplete and imperfect (and keep in mind, *everyone's* life is incomplete and imperfect!), but it's still a life. *Your* life. God's gift to you.

Even though Hannah might have been tempted to stay home from the trek to Shiloh every year, she probably needed the break from the mundane rhythm of daily life. Surely there were some joyous traditions she enjoyed along the way: Nights around campfires, singing and telling stories. Sweet moments with Elkanah, the husband who loved her, empty arms, broken womb, damaged heart, and all.

During one of my waiting seasons, I took up new hobbies to keep life interesting. I tried crocheting and knitting. (More accurately, I *failed* crocheting and knitting.) I got a dog. Competed in triathlons. Dabbled in gardening. Wrote a novel, and rediscovered my love of writing. I bought—wait for it—an oboe.

You should have witnessed the conversation when I told my husband, Kevin:

> Me (*to Kevin, quietly*): I want to get an oboe.
> Kevin (*not looking up from his computer*): Mm-hmm. Good. You should help a hobo.
> Me (*louder*): I *said*, I want to get an *oboe*.
> Kevin (*snort-laughing*): A *what*? Oh, yeah, the weird instrument? The one you used to play in middle and high school that sounds like a dying duck? That would be hilarious. Good one.
> Me: (*Awkward silence.*)
> Kevin (*looking up and seeing hurt all over my face*): Oh, you were serious?
> Me: Um, yeah.
> Kevin: (*Sits there for five minutes trying to arrange his face into a supportive expression.*)

But two weeks later, I was the proud (*proud* meaning "kind of embarrassed") owner of a used oboe. I can only imagine the thoughts going through Kevin's beleaguered brain as he handed over the money, the words he had to fight not to say out loud: "Hi, Music Store Owner. This is keep-my-wife-happy-so-she-doesn't-mope-around-the-house money. It's all yours."

But you know what? I enjoyed picking up an old skill. I even performed a few times at church. It was good for me to find joy in a new (old) skill and to find fresh purpose for something I'd loved to do in the past.

Don't just sit around waiting for the life you want; fill the days you have. Try new things. Take new risks. Remain social. Get out of the house. Keep your life fun and interesting.

Survival Skill Number Five: Show Up for Self-Reflection

"Don't waste your suffering." I have heard this said by a number of godly women I respect, and what wisdom it is.

Waiting is a form of suffering. And like it or not, it's an opportunity to grow—an opportunity we would not choose for ourselves, but an opportunity nonetheless.

We all have watched waiting destroy people—steal dreams, harden hearts, strangle joy. It transforms their entire personalities, making them bitter, envious, and jaded. They start stiff-arming the people who love them, and before long they are angry with God, alone in the crowd. They spend so much time asking *Why?* and *Why me?* and *How long?*—all questions without answers that lead only to anger and frustration—that they forget about the real issues, the questions they can answer, the answers they can choose: *How will I use this time?* and *Who will I become while I wait?*

But we have seen other people grow—even flourish—through seasons of waiting. Maybe they didn't want to ride this particular roller coaster, but they are strapped in and the ride has started, and they can't get off till it ends. . .so they find a way to enjoy it. They keep their eyes open, wave their hands around a bit, and get the full experience. They don't just *survive* the ride; they *live* it.

Seasons of waiting are a great time to start journaling. (I know, all the math- and science-brained people just had a minor panic attack. Apologies.) Journaling doesn't come naturally to everybody, but it's worth a try. I predict you will find it a source of relief, a place to vent, question, and process. At the end of every chapter, you will find journal prompts. If you aren't already doing so, try *writing down* your answers to the questions (the physical act of writing will help you to think on a deeper level and make connections you might not make by just sitting and pondering). Even if you don't usually love writing, I think you'll find that journaling ministers to you during waiting seasons, that it does something healing to your heart.

For starters, try writing down answers to questions like these:

- What does the Bible teach me about God's character
  that is still true even while I'm waiting?
- How do I see God taking care of me while I'm waiting?
- If I could change one thing about how I'm handling
  this waiting season, what would it be?

Survival Skill Number Six: Show Up to Serve

We won't camp out on this point because we have a whole chapter devoted to finding purpose during in-between times (chapter 10), but serving can redeem your season of waiting. If you can find a place to give or a person who needs you, you won't get sucked into the trap of selfishness and self-pity that Satan has laid for you. Your days will have meaning; your life will hold joy. Lose your life through service and sacrifice, and you might just find yourself along the way (Luke 9:24).

Survival Skill Number Seven: Don't Show Up to Social Media as Often

Transcript of a recent conversation between me and my sister, who is suffering through her own agonizing baby-wait, complete with weekly humiliations in paper gowns:

> Alexandra: Everyone I know is pregnant.
> Me: Have you thought about editing your newsfeed and
> blocking pregnancy stories?
> Alexandra, three days later: I now have only two people left
> in my newsfeed—Uncle Dave and Dad's seventy-
> year-old friend, Jack. They go to the doctor almost
> as often as I do.
> Me: *Laughing. Crying. Laugh-crying.*

Listen, friend, this is just practical advice, one waiter to another: There's nothing wrong with social media, but when you're waiting, social media is probably not the best place to spend all your spare time. Not unless you have a spiritual superpower that makes you immune to envy. I'm not saying you need to add complete social media deprivation to your list of afflictions, but you may need to take some breaks for sanity's sake, or at least take social media in smaller doses.

The day you find out you didn't get into the college or grad school you wanted? Not the day to torment yourself with everyone else's "look at me wearing my school T-shirt" updates.

The day The Guy ignores you for the eight hundredth day in a row? Not the day to go ~~sob~~ scroll through pictures of all your friends looking all cute and couple-y with their boyfriends.

The day your adoption proceedings suffer another delay? Not the time to suffer through friends' Instagram pictures of their adorable children.

During times like this, opt for face-to-face friendship instead of Facebook friendship. Seek the company of friends over the phone or in person instead of seeking comfort in social media connections. Just be smart. You know your own heart, your own struggles, and what you can handle without flushing your smartphone down the toilet.

Your social life won't go down in flames if you take a few weeks off of social media—or even if you decide to sign off altogether for a season. *Really.* You will still have friends, you will still have fun, and you will still find ways to learn what is going on in the world.

Survival Skill Number Eight: Show Up to Laugh

Waiting stinks. (Duh.) We've established that. And you will have dark days. We've established that.

But *keep laughing.*

Let's revisit Amber's story, backing up to her prebreakup days. Every moment with The Boy feels like a perfect proposal opportunity. She keeps her nails perfect, hair curled, makeup fresh. Makes a secret Pinterest wedding board.

They attend a mutual friend's wedding—*ooh! a proposal on the way home from a wedding could be super sweet!*—and this scene plays out:

DJ: "All right, all the single ladies on the dance floor for the bouquet toss!"

Laughing, Amber joins the jostling crowd of giggling girls.

Flowers fly.

Elbows fly.

Amber flies.

She lands triumphant, waving the bouquet and beaming. *It's a sign from God! I really am about to get engaged!* She turns to share a significant glance with her significant other and finds him frozen at the front of the crowd, staring at her with a look of abject horror on his face. Never in the history of commitment-phobia has a man's expression so clearly screamed *terrified of marriage; not even remotely ready to propose.* Confused and embarrassed, Amber creeps off the dance floor.

You know what got her through that night? Picturing her friends' faces when she told the story. Sure enough, the next day they made all the appropriate faces and sympathy sounds, and somehow they laughed about it. It was just *so awful* they had to laugh. (Amber and Mr. Afraid of Marriage broke up a few weeks later. She is now happily married to a man who is not afraid of marriage, though she waited several years to find him. She did not have a bouquet toss at her wedding.)

Laughing at yourself makes you feel less crazy. Finding humor in heartache brings healing. Tell your stories to friends who can help you find the funny in them. You'll feel better, I promise.

Waiting seasons don't have to be lost time, and they don't have to be the end of you. Expanding your spiritual survival skills will help you survive your trek through the barren places, however long, however winding. You might even make some happy memories along the way. But you can't make memories if you don't *go make them.* I pray that, like Hannah, you find courage to keep showing up to the places, people, and spiritual habits that can see you through day after day, month after month, even year after year. I pray that, like Hannah, blessing surprises you when you least expect it.

Waiting Room Reading

For Further Study
Hannah's story is found in 1 Samuel 1 and 2, and you can read about the life of her son, Samuel, in 1 Samuel 3–25.

Journal Prompt
1. What do you need to start showing up to again? Worship? Prayer? Fun? Self-reflection?
2. What fun or exciting things would you like to try during this waiting season? Are there any trips you'd like to take? Hobbies you'd like to pursue? New skills you'd like to develop?

Prayer Prompt
Guard me and deliver me;
do not let me be put to shame,
for I take refuge in You.
May integrity and what is right
watch over me,
for I wait for You.

God, redeem Israel, from all its distresses.
PSALM 25:20–22 HCSB

4
Lies about Waiting

Naomi's Story
Waiting to Die

Based on Ruth 1

*N*aomi's eyes scan the hills, feeling the hum of familiarity, the comforting sense of *home* after days traveling desert terrain. With every step, she has tried to convince herself, *Wait till we reach Bethlehem. Home will heal you.* But the rising swell of almost-joy fizzles, sinks before cresting. When she left Bethlehem forty years ago, she never could have imagined a homecoming like this: widowed, childless, alone. Alone but for her beloved daughter-in-law Ruth.

Make conversation, Naomi, she chides herself, feeling Ruth's anxious eyes on her, studying her. *Ruth needs it.*

"See that rock there?" she asks, pointing to a pockmarked boulder. "Maybe I'm imagining things, but I think we took a break there that first day—the day Elimelech and I took the boys and left for Moab." She forces brightness into the words, knowing Ruth needs the memory that causes Naomi so much pain. "We'd only ridden a short way, but Mahlon—he was only five then—was already whining, begging for water." As always, she senses Ruth's eager desperation, drinking in every detail about her dead husband, Naomi's youngest son, as if the stories could make him less dead. "Elimelech and I rested while the boys wrestled in the grass—they were like little lion cubs." A smile surprises her, and she stops talking, lost in memory.

> *"But Elimelech, how can you be so sure we'll be happy there, with so much unknown?"*
> *His strong arm draws her in close; his lips brush*

soft against her forehead. "Because I know the only thing that matters: we'll be together."

To-ge-ther, to-ge-ther. Her feet mock the words.

A boy jogs into view. Ruth hails him, presses a coin into his palm, exchanges words Naomi's dull ears cannot hear. When she turns back, Ruth's face is eager, coaxing. Naomi tries to summon a meager smile. "The boy will tell everyone we're coming," Ruth says. "He'll find your—our—family." The boy sprints toward town, his agile feet leaving little puffs of dust behind.

"Will they like me, do you think?" Ruth says so quietly Naomi wonders if she meant to speak aloud.

Naomi makes her voice firm. "Daughter, my family will love you as much as I do." But anxiety squirms, snakelike, in her gut: *What if there's no one left? No one to remember me, to take us in?*

As the road crests, the town comes into view, spread out on the side of a rocky, grass-splotched hill like a brown-and-green quilt. "Bethlehem!" says Ruth, a hitch of excitement in her voice. Naomi's heart flutters at the familiar sight: dusty houses clustered close, sharing secrets; scrubby trees tucked in tight, listening in.

Minutes later, the first running figures appear, their colorful clothing bright polka dots against the tawny backdrop. The children reach them first, flushed and tongue-tied, giggling and waving shyly until their mothers and grandmothers catch up in a swirl of skirts and excited chatter. Naomi scans faces with anxious eyes, seeking someone—anyone—she once knew.

The crowd parts. Two women, their faces bearing the tracks of time, hobble through, linked at the elbow. Their words weave on top of each other, braiding together in a tangle so Naomi can't tell which one is speaking. "Let us through—she's our cousin—our friend—we will know—"

A grin sneaks onto Naomi's face. "Rachel and Anna, I should have known you'd still be trying to outtalk each other after all these years."

Together they cry, "Naomi! It *is* you!"

And she is swept into a four-armed hug, nearly suffocated by the affection of old friends. At last they pull back to study each other.

"You've changed, cousin," Anna says, wagging a thick finger at Naomi's nose.

"So have you," Naomi says, pulling back from the finger, fighting tears and smiles, not sure which will win. "You've grown shorter."

"So have you, sweet Naomi," Rachel says. "So have we all. Just wait till the others see you—Sarah and Edith and Abigail—even Mary—all still living. *So long* we've wondered how you were, when you would return, *if* you would return."

A young woman steps forward. From a red wrapping on her chest, a baby's curious black eyes peep out, dark jewels winking in bright sun. The woman gives Ruth a shy smile and places a hand on Rachel's shoulder. "Mother, aren't you going to introduce us?"

Rachel draws herself up as tall as she can, proud smile shining. "Naomi, this is my Hadassah—my youngest, born two years after you left—and this little one, Joshua, is my tenth grandchild." Naomi reaches a finger out to stroke the baby's soft cheek.

Naomi raises her chin and steps back. "And this is my daughter-in-law Ruth." She feels Ruth's fingers lacing between hers, giving a squeeze, offering strength for the explanations they both dread. Naomi seeks the words, so hard to say. She sees Rachel's and Anna's eyes combing the road behind them. Again their words intertwine, asking the same question different ways: "Elimelech, Mahlon, Kilion, are they—behind? Bringing your animals, and children, and. . . ?"

Naomi shakes her head, feeling the sorrow swell and crash inside, given fresh strength on this familiar soil. She had hoped she would salvage joy, find relief from grief at the sight of home and friends, but now she knows: nothing has changed. "All gone," she whispers. "Buried in Moab, that cursed land." And in the saying of it, the out-loud speaking, the truth takes on fresh horror, the scab tears off the wound. She bleeds.

Ruth's arm finds her shoulders.

"Naomi!" Rachel and Anna speak at once, their eyes mirrors of sadness. Behind them, all the faces offer sympathy, compassion, pity.

The baby makes a feeble cry. Rachel and Anna step forward, as if for a hug.

Naomi's harsh voice is a slap against the space between them. "Don't call me that!" The women freeze, arms outstretched and uncertain. "There is nothing *Naomi*—nothing *pleasant*—in my life anymore." She feels Ruth's arm twitch against her shoulders, knows she has hurt her, but it's too late. The flood of caustic words, now released, cannot be dammed. "Call me *Mara*," she says, "because my life is bitter, and the hand of the Lord has gone out against me." Her eyes skip across the sad faces. "I left you full; I come back empty."

Anna steps forward to place one hand on Naomi's forearm. "Come live with me. We will be your family once more, Naomi."

"*Mara*," Naomi snaps, more angrily than she intends. Hurt flickers across Anna's face.

"Just wait. . .Mara," Rachel says, the name falling stiffly from her lips, "you will find joy once more, here with us. You will see. Just you wait."

Naomi-Mara feels a laugh jerk hard out of her chest. "There is no happiness left for me. Not so for Ruth—I intend to help her find new life here—but I wait only to die. Death will set me free."

Maybe your life isn't as bleak as Naomi's—but then, maybe it is. When first we meet her, Naomi isn't waiting for blessing anymore; she waits only to be released from grief. Heart broken, dreams stolen. To lose a husband and two sons before their time is a sorrow beyond words. The future she once envisioned has died, buried with her beloved, and now hope, too, has died, strangled by Satan's lies. You can hear the Enemy's evil manipulations, hissing beneath her own words to friends: "The Lord's hand has turned against me. . . . The Almighty has made my life very bitter. I went away full, but the Lord has brought me back empty. . . . The Lord has afflicted me; the Almighty has brought misfortune upon me" (Ruth 1:13, 20–21).

When we are waiting, life can feel empty. There's a void where *it* should be. We try to fill ourselves up, keep busy, but still the emptiness yawns, begging to be filled. And in that void, Satan starts to whisper.

When we are waiting, we feel vulnerable, weak, exposed. Our confidence may be down, our faith wavering, and the Enemy loves to exploit those weaknesses, slipping poisonous words through cracks in our armor. Jesus warned us about the words of Satan: "When he lies, he speaks his native language, for he is a liar and the father of lies" (John 8:44).

Satan has a particular set of lies he has designed to torment us during waiting seasons. His deceptions target us where it hurts the most: insecurities in our relationship with God and insecurities about ourselves—our own spirituality, faithfulness, or worthiness. Because the Enemy's words often ring with an element of truth, they are more difficult to fight. The trouble is, his lies often come with a scripture attached—a misunderstood scripture. They *seem* biblically sound, so we believe them. Just as Satan did with Jesus in the desert, he twists the truth so it *almost* sounds right.

What are the lies Satan tells us during our waiting seasons? They are not unlike the lies he told Naomi, lies that convinced her to abandon her joy, her name, herself, and take up the name Mara (meaning "bitter"). Let's dissect some of these lies in light of scripture and the big picture. Some of these lies bring up thorny theological topics, not easily explained or quickly defined. Here I offer my humble take on some tricky topics, with the hope that you will be inspired to study deep and think hard, not settling for easy, cliché answers to complex questions.

Before we start in on the actual *lies* about waiting, we have to address this humdinger of a statement: *God is doing this because...* (fill in the blank).

We need to begin here because we have all spoken sentences that start this way. And this phrase isn't a lie so much as a dangerous statement. Why? Because it assumes we can read God's mind. Anytime we find ourselves attempting to interpret God's thoughts or actions, we have to tread carefully and with humility.

> *"For my thoughts are not your thoughts,*
> *neither are your ways my ways,"*

declares the LORD.
"As the heavens are higher than the earth,
so are my ways higher than your ways
and my thoughts than your thoughts."

ISAIAH 55:8–9

God thinks differently than we do. Anytime we start playing the interpretation game, thinking things like "God is doing this because He thinks. . ." or "This is happening because God wants. . . " we should proceed with caution. Because unless God sends us a direct message from heaven, we are just guessing. We don't really know what God has in mind or why He does what He does. We can't know such things! During confusing times, we have to trust what the Bible tells us about God's nature, His grace, and His priorities, and choose to view our circumstances in light of those truths.

Well-meaning friends may offer explanations to make us feel better about our waiting times, and while their words come from a good place, a desire to comfort or help, let's be careful not to take speculation as gospel truth. Solomon writes in Ecclesiastes 8:17: "No one can comprehend what goes on under the sun. Despite all their efforts to search it out, no one can discover its meaning. Even if the wise claim they know, they cannot really comprehend it." I don't say this to suggest that people can't offer wisdom to help us work through our waiting times; I only want to warn against trying to read God's mind.

You will see where this mind reading can take us as we explore some of the specific lies Satan loves to tell:

God is making me wait because He is punishing me.

Sound familiar? It seems Naomi succumbed to this one when she said, "The Lord's hand has turned against me."

This lie can take several other related forms:

This is happening because I am in trouble with God.
God is holding out because I have done something wrong.

God is making me wait because I'm in sin and I'm not worthy.

God hasn't given me the blessing I seek because I don't deserve it (but everyone else does).

It's my fault God is making me wait.

Friend, Satan has whispered all of these lies to me (plus a few creative variations on the theme), and the more I have believed him, the more confident he has become, his whispers turning to shouts that taunted me even in my dreams.

Satan means "Accuser." One of Satan's favorite roles is as prosecuting attorney, putting us on trial before God, hurling our own sins and weaknesses in our faces. But let me tell you something, and please listen and try to hear—really hear—and believe: *When life gets hard, it doesn't mean God is punishing you.*

For starters, let's consider the godly (but imperfect) men and women we are encountering in the pages of this book: Naomi, Ruth, David, Joseph, Sarah, Miriam. . . All suffered. All waited. All lost things, and people, along the way. Jesus Himself lived a hard life filled with suffering. But do we look at their sorrows, their waiting seasons, and think, *They deserved what they got. They brought it upon themselves?* Of course not!

God's people have long misinterpreted difficulty as a sign of God's displeasure or punishment. Barrenness was often seen as a sign of hidden sin, and women who could not conceive were viewed not with the pity and compassion they needed, but with mistrust and accusation. Illness was viewed in a similar way. As if suffering people's grief and loss were not enough, now guilt and shame were added to their pain. But time and again in the Bible, we see that this was a man-made concept, not from God. In Luke, God goes out of His way to point out a barren couple's blamelessness in their heartbreaking situation. He introduces Zechariah and Elizabeth like this: "Both of them were righteous in the sight of God, observing all the Lord's commands and decrees blamelessly. But they were childless because Elizabeth was not able to conceive" (1:6–7). Similarly, the Bible does not criticize or blame other women who experienced long barren stretches: Sarah, Hannah, Rebekah, Rachel. They are not pictured as perfect people, but neither are they *blamed* for their situations.

Jesus roundly rejects *suffering-is-your-fault* theology in John 9, when his disciples ask, "Rabbi, who sinned, this man or his parents, that he was born blind?" "Neither this man nor his parents sinned," said Jesus, "but this happened so that the works of God might be displayed in him" (verses 2–3). Jesus, being God's Son, had authority you and I don't possess to "read God's mind," interpreting God's will and intention in this man's situation. To prove that authority, Jesus promptly healed the man, revealing His own divinity and fulfilling God's plan.

I suspect we get hung up on the thought of waiting as a punishment because the Old Testament does contain examples of God disciplining His people, even making them wait, when they sinned—most notably the Israelites' forty-year desert vacation. We read their stories and think, *The Israelites suffered as punishment for their sins; therefore, anytime I suffer, I must also have sinned.*

But we have to be careful not to take theological leaps. We can't always apply Bible stories *directly* to our own situations, like so: "I'm wandering in a time of confusion in my life, feeling directionless and unsure, so I, too, must be under the punishment of God." Keep in mind that when God disciplined or punished His people in the Old Testament, He usually sent prophets to give clear warnings about specific offenses (idol worship, immorality, deliberate disobedience, and so on). During the Exodus, the people had Moses speaking words straight from God, and they defied God's instructions (Numbers 13–14). Before God's people were sent into exile in Babylon, God went to great trouble for many years, sending prophets—Isaiah, Jeremiah, and others—to warn them exactly what they were doing wrong and exactly what would happen if they didn't change. He gave them *decades' worth* of opportunities to repent (2 Chronicles 36:15–21).

And while we should learn from mistakes that God's people have made in the past and heed warnings we find in the Bible's cautionary tales, we must be careful not to assume that God will deal with you and me in exactly the same way. For one thing, you and I are individuals, not nations. God tends to deal with individuals differently than He dealt with the nation of Israel as a whole. For another thing, I have never had a prophet show up to my house with a personal prophecy just for me: "Unless you change xyz, you will never find true love. . . . Unless you change xyz, you will never publish a novel." For a third thing, God has employed some different methods since Jesus came offering grace and the indwelling Spirit freely to all who follow Him (before Christ, the average follower of God did not have the Holy Spirit). While we see concepts of direct punishment throughout the Old Testament, God's people are now united as a church, not a country. Since Jesus established the church, God is more than our King, and we—body of Christ, family of God—are more than a nation.

Granted, our sins can bring pain, suffering, and tragedy into our lives. Poor choices can delay blessings. But chances are, if you are in that boat, you *know* exactly what went wrong, and when. Those kinds of big-consequence sins are generally hard to miss. (And remember, even if you are experiencing long-term consequences from past sins, those sins can still be completely forgiven, washed in the blood of Christ.)

Let's come up for air here and get a little more practical. Let's look at some scriptures, considering the nature of God and His relationship to us.

> *The LORD is compassionate and gracious,*
> *   slow to anger, abounding in love.*
> *He will not always accuse,*
> *   nor will he harbor his anger forever;*
> *he does not treat us as our sins deserve*
> *   or repay us according to our iniquities.*
> *For as high as the heavens are above the earth,*
> *   so great is his love for those who fear him;*
> *as far as the east is from the west,*
> *   so far has he removed our transgressions from us.*
> *As a father has compassion on his children,*

> so the LORD has compassion on those who fear him;
> for he knows how we are formed,
> he remembers that we are dust.
>
> PSALM 103:8–14

This gorgeous psalm reminds us of the height, depth, and breadth of God's grace. He is slow to anger and has more love than He knows what to do with. He does not treat us as our sins deserve. Sure, we all deserve to be alienated from God because of our sins, but thanks to the blood of Christ, we receive grace instead. God, like a good father, knows our weaknesses and doesn't hold them against us. Grace is not a temporary, transient position based on our day-to-day performance. When we become Christians, grace is a place we *stand* (Romans 5:2). Because of Jesus, Christians are invited to "approach God's throne of grace *with confidence*" (Hebrews 4:16, emphasis added).

Grace. Don't be fooled by this short word, these five letters—so small, so unassuming—for *grace* may be the most powerful word in the world. God's grace can take our ugliest messes—harshest words, cruelest thoughts, most shameful deeds—and wash us clean. Not just it's-been-washed-but-I-can-still-see-the-coffee-stain clean. No, we get bright white, as-if-it's-never-been-worn clean.

God's grace is big enough.

God's grace lasts long enough.

God's grace never runs dry.

Waiting is not a punishment from God; it is a part of life. Everyone waits for things, even the most righteous of people.

God is making me wait because He is mad at me.

This lie is a first cousin of the *God-is-punishing-me* lie, but it deserves its own discussion. Early in our marriage, I sometimes convinced myself that Kevin was upset with me. Maybe he was quieter than usual or seemed preoccupied or forgot to kiss me before he left the house. In my mind, his silence was a condemnation: *I've done something wrong. He's mad.* The funny thing is, Kevin is an easygoing guy who hardly ever gets angry or even annoyed—but still, insecurity and imagination could join forces to make me paranoid. If I fully went down the rabbit hole, I might torture myself for hours, inventing a list of a thousand things he *might* be upset about. And every time, when I finally stopped sitting alone in my tormented thoughts and just asked him, "Hey, are we okay? Are you upset about something?" he would look at me like I was bonkers and say something like, "We're great! I love you! I was just thinking about the Duke game."

We have all known passive-aggressive people who get angry but won't tell us why they're mad. They stonewall us and shut us out, or they make sarcastic, cutting, vaguely critical remarks and wait for us to interpret. We are hurt and mystified, wondering: *What did I do wrong?* God simply does not operate the way people do.

I can't read God's mind, but I do know what the Bible tells us about His character, and based on the picture the Bible paints, I can tell you this: God is probably not making you wait because He is angry. God is gracious, not one to hold a grudge. He speaks clearly when He wants us to change. He speaks through His Word, His people, and our consciences.

"But," you say, "I *feel* so guilty—so I must *be* guilty."

All right, my fellow guilt-plagued friend. Let's take a detour here to deal with this thoroughly and set you free from your misery. God gave us consciences to nudge us toward change when sin crops up in our lives. But some of us have a tough time distinguishing between true guilt and vague feelings that are nothing more than false accusations from Satan. When we are feeling guilty, we have to figure out if our consciences are telling us it's time to make a change or if our consciences are too sensitive.

If you can't shake the idea that God is making you wait because sin is hiding somewhere in your heart, here is what I suggest: Give yourself a specific time limit, a few days or a week at most, to think and pray and get resolved inside. Within that time frame, examine yourself. Ask God to help you see yourself clearly. You might borrow David's prayer from Psalm 139:23–24:

> *Search me, God, and know my heart;*

test me and know my anxious thoughts.
See if there is any offensive way in me,
and lead me in the way everlasting.

Rest assured that God loves you enough to show you things you need to change. Compare your life with God's Word, asking yourself if there is some obvious sin you haven't dealt with. By "obvious sin," I mean something that doesn't line up with the Bible's clear commands: for example, you are holding on to bitterness, or committing sexual sin, or living in deceit.

If you realize you need to make some changes, ask God and spiritual friends to help you begin working on that area of your life. If you find sin, confess it, repent, accept grace, and move on: "Therefore confess your sins to each other and pray for each other so that you may be healed" (James 5:16). But understand this: even if you do find some sin in your life, chances are you haven't been made to wait because God is angry with you.

If, at the end of the time frame you have set, your heart check doesn't reveal any obvious sin, then please *let yourself relax and enjoy the grace of God.* Stop blaming yourself for your wait. Trusting in the love and grace of God takes faith.

God doesn't want me to be happy.

I suspect Naomi believed this lie when she said, "The Almighty has made my life very bitter." This issue has cropped up in my prayers during times of intense frustration: "God, why, why, why are You holding out on this when You know how happy it will make me? Do You *want* me to feel frustrated and unfulfilled? Do You hate it when I'm happy?" I know. Yikes.

We should start by observing this: It *is* true that God is more concerned with our holiness than with our temporary happiness. It is also true that sometimes things that make us holy also make us unhappy for a time. Suffering can make us holier. Sorrow for sin can make us holier. Self-denial can make us holier. None of those things are particularly fun experiences. Now, as a parent, I get this concept: I want my kids to be happy, but I am *more* concerned with their character. I also know that sometimes they need to hear *no* and suffer temporary unhappiness for various reasons that are good for them in the long run.

But does it follow that God wants us to be *un*happy? That He makes us wait just to watch us squirm?

Absolutely not. Jesus is clear on this in Matthew 7:9–11:

> *"Which of you, if your son asks for bread, will give him*
> *a stone? Or if he asks for a fish, will give him a snake?*
> *If you, then, though you are evil, know how to give good*
> *gifts to your children, how much more will your Father*
> *in heaven give good gifts to those who ask him!"*

Isaiah puts it this way:

> *Yet the* LORD *longs to be gracious to you;*
>   *therefore he will rise up to show you compassion.*
> *For the* LORD *is a God of justice.*
>   *Blessed are all who wait for him!*

> *People of Zion, who live in Jerusalem, you will weep no*
> *more. How gracious he will be when you cry for help! As*
> *soon as he hears, he will answer you.*
> ISAIAH 30:18–19

God is making me wait because He doesn't want me to have The Thing I want.

This one can also sound like this:

> *The waiting must be a sign. I'm not meant to have The Thing I want.*
> *The waiting must be a sign. This must not be God's will for me.*

Here we are with more mind reading. We Christians can be superstitious, seeing signs and messages in everything. Again, let's be careful with assumptions like these, because they can make us feel guilty for still wanting The Thing after a long delay. They can discourage us from persevering. Until you get a final *no*, an absolute closed door, then you don't have a clear word from the Lord.

It's not wrong to keep asking, keep seeking, keep knocking. You are not resisting the will of God by being persistent, by continuing to seek a desire long delayed. (Keep in mind that the opposite also holds true: If you decide, after a long wait, to move on and set your desires on other things, you are free to do so. It's not wrong to let go even before you get a definitive *no* from God.)

If I don't wait perfectly, God will never give me what I want.

This lie goes hand in hand with its cousin: *I won't get what I want till I have enough faith.* (See chapter 9 for a more detailed exploration of faith and doubt.)

This kind of thinking puts a lot of pressure on us and on our performance. It views waiting seasons as tests from God. He is up there with His celestial red pen, marking papers, and we suspect He is secretly itching to put a big fat F at the top of the page. Every time we stumble or doubt, we panic: "Did I just cross the line and blow my chance? Now I'll *never* get that prayer answered!"

We are not going to do the "does God test people" topic complete justice here because it's complicated, but a fair, brief summary would be this: Yes, God sometimes tests us (Deuteronomy 13:3; 1 Chronicles 29:17). But by *God tests us*, we don't mean He puts us through trials to see if we will fail (even secretly hoping we will fail). No, when God tests us, He is looking to find out what is in our hearts. He is looking to expose strength and weakness, to show us where we are and where we need to grow. His tests are not so much like a driver's license exam—you pass or fail—but like the diagnostic tests a car manufacturer does on the cars themselves before releasing them into the world. The manufacturer needs to know if the vehicles are safe and ready for the road or if they need more work before they leave the factory.

Now, let's move on to the question about whether we can be blessed even if we struggle during our waiting seasons. Let's compare finishing a waiting season to graduating from college: as we say here in the South, some people graduate summa cum laude, some magna cum laude, some "Thank the Lawd-y." You don't have to get a 4.0 in college to graduate. You can fail some tests, even flunk a course or two, and still get your diploma. Are there some benefits and opportunities that sometimes go along with a high GPA? Sure. Is that an accomplishment to be proud of? Sure. But we celebrate every graduate's achievement even if she only made it by the hair of her chinny-chin-chin. The point is, she made it. She worked hard, and she *didn't quit*. She made it to the end.

Like all analogies, this one is imperfect, but I hope it sheds some light on how God looks at our "performance" during waiting seasons. God doesn't expect perfection. Of course He is happy when we remain faithful, righteous, and close to Him (and when we do those things, we may experience some benefits, like peace and growth and joy), but God understands that we all struggle, and even fall flat, during our waiting times. Naomi grew bitter for a while, and yet she survived her waiting season—even came through it with great joy and blessing. God's biggest concern is that we *don't quit*. That we make it to the end, *thank the Lawd-y*.

The Thing Everyone Says That Might Not Be True

Let's move away from lies about waiting to address one final problematic sentence, a line you have probably heard—maybe even told yourself—eight thousand times since you started waiting. Ready? Here goes: *It will happen at the right time.*

I know. Some of you reading this just did a double take: "Is she really saying that 'It will happen at the right time' isn't true?"

Maybe. Sorta-kinda. I'm not saying it's a lie, but I am saying it's complicated. Hang with me while we hash this one out. You might not land in the same place as I have on this question—and I have agonized over it for years—but it's worth a discussion.

Before we dive in, let me say this: I know many people find the thought *It will happen at the right time* to be a great comfort in times of waiting. It helps them let go and give control over to God. Truly, friend, I don't mean to take away a source of peace and comfort but to point you to a perspective I believe will ultimately be even more comforting, because it's empowering. It shows you that your prayers matter. Your opinion and desires count. Your choices and actions make a difference. You are not just a passive victim of God's choices from on high; you are an active participant *with your heavenly Father* in determining your future. God makes the ultimate decisions, of course, but He very much cares about what you want.

Okay, let's take a closer look. *It will happen at the right time.* First difficulty: this statement assumes The Thing *will* happen, and we will get what we want. We have to accept that we don't know the future and we might get a *no.*

Second, we need to be careful throwing this sentence around to ourselves and to other people who are waiting. During my various waiting days, I have heard this line from a gazillion people, all trying to help me feel better and find peace. Honestly, they didn't help me feel better—I felt angry and frustrated: *God is doing this to me on purpose! Aaahhh!* This line sent my faith into a tailspin. (I can't blame people for my own sinful feelings, of course, but that's how I reacted.)

I think this line holds power because people tend to read too much into passages inadvertently wrested from their intended context, particularly these two:

> *"From one man he made all the nations, that they should inhabit the whole earth; and he marked out their appointed times in history and the boundaries of their lands."*
>
> ACTS 17:26

> *Your eyes saw me when I was formless; all my days were written in Your book and planned before a single one of them began.*
>
> PSALM 139:16 HCSB

Some people read these brief passages and conclude that God has *every detail* of our lives, our "appointed times in history," already mapped out. All our days have been preplanned, written in God's book, down to the finest detail. Every event in our lives is supposed to happen at a single perfect, predetermined time.

But is that really what these passages are saying? *Every detail* preplanned, *all timing* preordained? Keep in mind that the second passage is poetry, meant to be read differently than prose.

While we should give God full credit for being all-powerful, all-knowing, and all-wise, and for having meaningful involvement in our lives, the Bible also indicates that God gives us a say in our own lives. We are not His robots, slaves, or pawns. Is there an ideal, perfect time for every event in our lives? Maybe. Maybe not. But consider this: Even if there *is* an ideal time for life events, sometimes *people's choices* (our own choices and those of others) affect the timeline. God allows us to make real, life-changing decisions, even sinful ones. Of course, God is powerful enough, and God is flexible enough, to work *with*, *through*, and even *around* human activity! (Remember Sarah and the Hagar Incident?) Romans 8:28 reassures us that even though not all things in our lives are good, God is ultimately able to *work for our good*, even through difficult and painful situations.

A great example of the complex relationship between divine intention and human intervention is Jesus' first miracle in John 2, where He turns water into wine at a wedding. Listen in on the borderline comical conversation between Jesus and Mary—the dialogue here is taken word for word from the NIV:

> Mary (*whispering to Jesus*): They have no more wine.
> Jesus (*whispering back to Mary*): Woman, why do
> you involve me? My hour has not yet come.
> Mary (*waving a dismissive hand and turning to the
> servants*): Do whatever he tells you.
> Jesus (*rolling up His sleeves with a half smile and an
> affectionate sigh*): Fill the jars with water.

Of course, I added in the whispering and the waving, the smile and the sigh. I picture Jesus heaving a tender, *Oh, Mother* kind of sigh, with a little shake of His head and an ironic half smile cast heavenward. We all know what it feels like when our mothers—er, *encourage* us—to do something before we are ready to do it. Jesus' time for revealing His miraculous powers had not yet come, and yet when His beloved mother intervened, Jesus—God in the flesh—honored her request and changed His timeline!

So what's my point in all this? I have several. Let's spell this out as clearly as possible:

It's complicated. Time and predetermined events are complex concepts, and let's take care not to apply easy "Band-Aid" answers to people's deep wounds.

We are not helpless. The wording "It will happen at the right time" is unfortunate because it promotes a feeling of helplessness, a sense that we are victims of God's preordained and inflexible choices for us. This concept also makes us feel like God has made up His mind already, so our prayers don't make a difference. There is no conversation; everything has already been decided for us.

Our actions and attitudes matter. When we tell ourselves *It will happen when it's supposed to happen*, we might feel discouraged from taking action. We might think, *God's going to do what He wants to do, when He wants to do it, no matter what I say or do.* We might think, *God has already decided if and when He is going to heal me, so why go to the doctor? Why eat right and take my medicine?* Or *If God has already decided if and when I'm going to overcome depression, then why should I seek counseling or treatment? God will just make it go away "at the right time."* Remember: God gives us a say, and He lets us influence His timeline for our lives.

Remember Who the Real Enemy Is

Did you notice a common theme threading through the lies we challenged in this chapter? All these lies are designed to make *God* seem like the enemy instead of Satan. These lies breed fear, mistrust, and discouragement. They make us insecure with God. Distant. Maybe even bitter, like Naomi. At a time when we most need our Father—we ache to curl up close and cry in His loving arms, to lie down and find rest in the protective shadow of His wings—we hesitate. We take a step back. Suspicion, guilt, and fear darken our view of God, damaging our trust. If the lies go unchecked long enough, we pull away. When that happens, Satan wins.

Let's fight back. Let's see through the lies. Your Father wants to walk your waiting days hand in hand, comforting you, lending you courage, carrying you when your strength gives out. Listen now to God's words, not Satan's:

> "Fear not, for I have redeemed you;
>   I have summoned you by name; you are mine.
> When you pass through the waters,
>   I will be with you;
> and when you pass through the rivers,
>   they will not sweep over you.
> When you walk through the fire,
>   you will not be burned;
>   the flames will not set you ablaze. . . .
> Since you are precious and honored in my sight,
>   and because I love you,
> I will give men in exchange for you."
>   ISAIAH 43:1–2, 4 NIV 1984

God sees. God hears. God cares.
And that's the truth.

Waiting Room Reading

For Further Study
Naomi's life story is told in the book of Ruth. If you wrestle with deep questions like the ones we tackled in this chapter, I recommend Philip Yancey's book *Prayer: Does It Make Any Difference?* (Zondervan, 2006).

Journal Prompt

Which of Satan's lies do you wrestle with most? Do you believe God loves you, likes you, and wants what is best for you? Have you been blaming yourself for your season of waiting? How does knowing that God is not angry with you, not punishing you, transform your view of waiting?

Prayer Prompt

But the eyes of the LORD are on those who fear him,
*   on those whose hope is in his unfailing love,*
to deliver them from death
*   and keep them alive in famine.*

We wait in hope for the LORD;
*   he is our help and our shield.*
In him our hearts rejoice,
*   for we trust in his holy name.*
May your unfailing love be with us, LORD,
*   even as we put our hope in you.*
PSALM 33:18–22

5
When Prayer Becomes a Battleground

David's Story
The Dreams We Had

Based on 1 Samuel 19:11–17 and Psalm 13

The cave floor is cool and hard. David sits alone, apart from his men, lyre in hand, singing a prayer as memories surge.

> *"This can't be happening," Michal said, pushing words past tears. David and Michal stood beside their bedroom window in the dark, studying shadows outside. Already night's stark black was softening. Dawn was coming, and with it, Saul's soldiers.*
>
> *David set down his pack and pulled his bride in close. Her curves still new to his arms. Her perfume—all flowers and sunshine—still dizzying. His blood kicked hard.*
>
> *"Just pray," he said, tangling fingers into her dark curls, drawing her nearer, breathing her in. "Pray that God will make your father see reason—that I have no desire to take over his throne, that I am no threat." He wiped a tear from her cheek with his thumb, memorizing the feel of her skin.*

He shuts his eyes against the memory, still too painful, too fresh, though it has been eight months. Eight eternal months since he has seen her, held her, heard her voice.

A different memory surfaces, an older one:

Oil ran down his ears, his cheeks, like tears. Still dazed, David blinked up at the old prophet Samuel standing in front of him with hands raised high. David almost said, "I don't want to be king. Did you come to the wrong house? Anoint the wrong son of Jesse?" But his brothers were cheering, his mother weeping, his father beaming, so he bit back the words.

Samuel's wrinkled hand rested warm on David's shoulder. "I'll be seeing more of you, son. You just wait: the Lord has a great plan for your life."

Aloud David says, "Is this what Samuel meant? Is *this* God's great plan?" His words bounce cold off cave walls, his castle. "Some king I have made," he mutters, summoning a limp smile.

He gives God his anguish, a strangled song:

"How long must I wrestle with my thoughts
and day after day have sorrow in my heart?
How long will my enemy triumph over me?
Look on me and answer, Lord my God."

The memory of Michal forces its way back, and he falters, loses the melody.

"Look on me and answer, my love," David said. "You are sure Saul will not harm you?"

Michal pushed small fists against his chest, lifting flushed cheeks and swollen eyes to meet his gaze. "My father will not harm me," she said, her voice firm. "But you. . . Promise me you'll stay alive. Promise you'll come back to me when Father relents." She ducked her face into his chest, muffling her words. "Promise we'll have babies and grow old together. Promise—"

"I promise," he whispered, "ten thousand times I promise." With one finger, he tipped her chin up, his lips finding hers for a kiss he promised himself would not be their last.

He takes a shuddering breath and sings a shaking plea:

"Give light to my eyes, or I will sleep in death,
and my enemy will say, 'I have overcome him,'
and my foes will rejoice when I fall."

"Don't fall," Michal said, gently pushing him toward the window. The sky had turned navy. "Hurry."

Hefting his body into the window, he perched for a moment on the ledge. Fear speared him: Would he ever come back? He took one last uncertain look around. A statue lay covered in his place on their bed. Goat hair poked out from beneath the blanket, a lame attempt to fool Saul's soldiers, buy David a few precious hours. He barked a laugh at the ridiculousness of it all.

"David, I—" Michal's voice stifled his laugh and stole back his gaze. "I'll wait for you. As long as it takes, I'll wait for you."

Fast he strums the lyre, heart quickening with the memory of joy, the confidence that God was—*still is*—with him. God gave him Michal. God gave him a promise. God would not fail.

"But I trust in your unfailing love;
my heart rejoices in your salvation."

"God save me," he prayed, and leapt from the window. On soft feet he landed. In the east, the sky was bleeding. He ran for the sun.

David shuts out the memory of pain and focuses on the oil dripping down, the prophet's promise proclaimed over his life, his future.

> "I will sing the Lord's praise,
> for he has been good to me."

Still strumming, still humming, he makes himself remember. Over and again he sings the line, louder and stronger, till his words and mind and heart are all in tune. God would keep His promise—David would wait. Michal would wait. God would be true.

David spent years in the wilderness hiding in caves, living among Israel's enemies, leading a band of ragged men. Waiting for relief, vindication, a normal life. Waiting for Samuel's prophecy, God's promise, to finally come true. Over the years, David became a master at bringing intense feelings to God and working through them in a righteous way. Heartache and hurt drove David closer to God, not farther away; disappointment and delay made him better, not bitter. His prayer life can teach us how to pray our way through the barren waiting times, no matter how many detours or setbacks we face along the way.

The Struggles

Prayer gets complicated when we are waiting. It goes like this: If we could have gotten The Thing we want for ourselves, we would have gotten it already—a long time ago. We have done what we can, as much as we can, but now it's up to God to give the final divine thumbs-up. When days stretch into months and months melt into years, feeling close to God, feeling heard and loved by Him, grows increasingly difficult.

When we are waiting long term for something, we face a unique set of struggles in our walk with God.

We may feel:

- vulnerable

- out of control
- ignored by God
- unimportant to God
- disliked by God
- insecure with God
- confused by God
- disappointed in God
- ambivalent toward God
- disciplined by God
- distant from God
- under a curse of God
- hurt by God
- disillusioned by God's promises
- resentful toward God
- sinful before God, searching our hearts for hidden sin
- guilty about how we feel toward God

Each of these emotions affects our prayer life in some way. I have experienced each one during waiting seasons—sometimes every one of them all at once. On those days, you might find my husband reorganizing the garage or "mowing the lawn" for eight hours straight. I'm no expert on lawn mowing, but I suspect eight hours is a bit much. I'm kidding—sort of. But on days when I let dark feelings descend, it's like walking around with my own personal rain cloud, keeping me in sadness and shadow all day. Even if I wanted to step into the light, I couldn't. When we feel distant from God, unloved by God, the world is a dim place indeed.

From Refuge to Battleground

The longer we have to wait, the more we may struggle in our prayer lives and in our attitudes toward God. Prayer, once a place of refuge, gradually begins to feel like a battleground: Our will resisting God's plan. Our plea rattling heaven's gates. We might even stop praying altogether.

Eleven years into my journey of seeking a break in my writing career, I could hardly pray. I had come so close—an editor had assured me she was *almost positive* we had a deal, the last meeting a mere technicality—but the deal fell through at the last minute. I sat on the floor of my bedroom and cried. My husband quietly took the kids out to dinner; friends mailed emergency chocolate.

When I finally got up off the floor, God and I had hit an impasse. I'd spent years positioning myself to write for a living, but now that the final *yes* rested in God's hands, it felt like He was refusing to give it. I couldn't find any new ways to say "please." So for a while there, I'd show up for my morning prayer time and just sit, saying silently to God, *Well, we both know what I have to say. Now it's Your turn.* I was frustrated, bewildered, hurt.

Sound familiar? Surely I'm not the only one. The longer we wait on an answer, the more distant God feels. His silence fuels our suspicions: *Does He even care? Is He unmoved by my tears, my pleas?* Just as in the garden, the evil snake whispers doubt through gaps in our shield of faith.

After a while, God may start to feel like the enemy. *The Great Giver? Yeah right. More like the Great Disappointer. The Great Withholder. He is holding out on me on purpose. Ignoring me. Torturing me. He doesn't want what's best for me. He probably doesn't even like me.*

We don't like to admit this, lest we get struck by lightning, but the truth is, some of us get mad at God. Bitterness begins to wrap icy tentacles around our hearts—suffocating hope, strangling trust—till only anger remains. And what a terrifying place that is, when you feel resentment toward God clouding your vision, darkening your heart: not only are you wandering in the unmarked wilderness, but now you have lost your compass.

In the middle of our baby-wait, my mother was diagnosed with multiple sclerosis. Our entire family was left reeling, terrified, while we waited to learn just how bad her diagnosis was—which kind of MS she had, what kind of suffering her future might hold. Even when we learned she had a milder version of the disease, every time she had another MRI we held our breath: *Was she getting worse?* It was one of those times when you half expect your brain and heart to explode from stress and fear.

One afternoon my husband, not knowing what to say or how to comfort me—about Mom, about the baby we couldn't have, about *all of it*—suggested we pray together. There on the floor of our guest room—the sad, sterile room that should have become a nursery long ago—we knelt and prayed. I don't remember what I said, but I was angry, and I didn't hold back. When I opened my eyes, my husband sat there blinking at me, shocked. I'm pretty sure he scooted a few inches away from me, in case God decided to take me out with my own personal tornado. Defensive, I snapped, "What? I'm telling God what I really feel!" We got up from our prayer, both of us feeling worse, not better. I walked away fearing that not only was I never going to become a mother, but now I was never going to make it to heaven either.

But you know what I now realize? I was on the right track, even if I had come close to crossing a line in that prayer.

The Psalms: Carving a Path through the Wilderness of Waiting

Thank goodness we are not the first of God's people to suffer through confusing times in our walks with God. Others before us, David chief among them, have also had to find a way to pray through pain.

God has devoted an entire book in His Word to prayers. When we read the book of Psalms, something in us rings with familiarity, echoes our own amen. The Psalms prompt our own prayers, offer words to borrow when we can't find our own.

And David—shepherd, songwriter, outlaw, king—was master of the psalmists. He authored about half of the 150 psalms in the Bible, and in them he gives voice to our struggles and fears. In Psalm 10:1 he cries, "Why, LORD, do you stand far off? Why do you hide yourself in times of trouble?" When I read these words, I get goose bumps: *Has he been spying on me, pulling secret thoughts from my head?*

> *I am feeble and utterly crushed;*
> *I groan in anguish of heart.*

All my longings lie open before you, Lord;
  my sighing is not hidden from you.
My heart pounds, my strength fails me;
  even the light has gone from my eyes.
My friends and companions avoid me because of my
wounds;
  my neighbors stay far away.

PSALM 38:8–11

At last, I think, *someone understands what I feel and has found a way to pray it.*

Prayers we hear in church can be scripted, formal, void of feeling. Not the Psalms. They introduce us—more, they *invite* us—to an entirely different kind of prayer. David and the other psalmists beg, plead, question, wonder, fear, lament, praise, rejoice, worry, anguish, mourn, celebrate, rant, curse, and bless. Their prayers run wild: unbridled, unashamed, sometimes even unrighteous. Freely they roam the full gamut of the human experience, soaring to heights of ecstatic joy, diving to depths of hopeless despair. They mirror our own doubt, despondency, fear, confusion, weariness, and sense of abandonment. Some lines are shocking: "May his children be fatherless and his wife a widow. May his children be wandering beggars; may they be driven from their ruined homes" (Psalm 109:9–10). Yikes. Who wrote those bitter lines, so laced with venom? David, the man after God's own heart (Acts 13:22)! He prayed vengeance on his enemies, and yet he still got to be king of Israel; he still got to go to heaven. (Maybe there's hope for you and me after all!)

And the thing is, God put those prayers in the Bible, and He didn't do it by accident. He didn't insert disclaimers or notes of clarification in the margins: *Note to people reading this psalm: This is not a prayer a righteous person should pray. It's here as a warning. If you pray this, you will immediately be obliterated by a fiery meteor.*

Nope. God has put them in there and let them stand uncensored, shaking their fists, stark and hateful, red slashes of fury that bleed across the softer hues of grace and gratitude.

Why?

Because God is saying, *"I get it—all of it. The full scope of your emotion, righteous and unrighteous. I want to hear about it. I can take it."*

God is inviting us to pray *real prayers*. To bring everything to Him—to bring *ourselves* to Him. He wants to hear us out. He can handle it.

If you are suffering through a bleak waiting season and you have hit a wall in your prayer life, borrow the Psalms. Listen as they whisper (and sometimes shout) your own fears. Find comfort in knowing you are not alone. Let the psalmists speak to your tears and give voice to your hurts.

Try these out for starters:

> *Have mercy on me, LORD, for I am faint;*
>> *heal me, LORD, for my bones are in agony.*
> *My soul is in deep anguish.*
>> *How long, LORD, how long?*

> *Turn, LORD, and deliver me;*
>> *save me because of your unfailing love. . . .*

> *I am worn out from groaning.*

> *All night long I flood my bed with weeping*
>> *and drench my couch with tears.*
> *My eyes grow weak with sorrow.*
>>>>> PSALM 6:2–4, 6–7

> *My God, my God, why have you forsaken me?*
>> *Why are you so far from saving me,*
>> *so far from my cries of anguish?*
> *My God, I cry out by day, but you do not answer,*
>> *by night, but I find no rest.*
>>>>> PSALM 22:1–2

God invites us to pray prayers like these. Even Jesus, in His final hours on the cross, borrowed from David's psalms to express the anguish He felt when God, having placed the sins of the world on Jesus' head, had to withdraw His presence: "My God, my God, why have you forsaken me?" (Matthew 27:46; cf. Psalm 22:1).

Let us learn from David and from Jesus to pray prayers that peel the paint off the walls. Prayers that strip our souls bare. Prayers that leave us limp on the floor, emptied of words.

Gethsemane Prayers

My mom has often told me the story of one of her most painful prayers—she calls it her "Gethsemane prayer." She had been dating a guy for about two years, and she was sure a ring was coming soon. Instead, he pulled her aside one day and laid this one on her: "You know you're my first girlfriend ever, and now I'm worried that we got too serious too fast and I should have dated other people. There's this other girl I met, and I think I need to take her out to be sure. I need your permission to be sure."

I know. Here's the part where we all want to throw a brick at him, because my mom is the sweetest, most delightful soul ever to grace this planet. But my mom, being wise beyond her twenty-one years, swallowed her tears and said, "Sure, go ahead and take her out." Because she knew she did not want to marry a guy who wasn't crazy in love with her even if she was crazy in love with him. It's no fun being crazy in love all by yourself. She either wanted him *sure*—and not just matter-of-fact sure; she wanted "You are the greatest woman in the universe, and I will never even blink at another woman as long as I live" sure—or not at all.

But she went home and got on her face and prayed all night. In that prayer, she gave the relationship over to God. She begged God to work and to clarify and to ~~hit her boyfriend in the head with a hammer~~ help her boyfriend think clearly. To either help him realize he was madly, greatest-woman-in-the-universe in love with her, or to help her let go. She prayed and surrendered her future to God's loving hands, knowing that even if her boyfriend let her down, God never would. In the morning, she got up red-eyed and exhausted but at peace.

The boyfriend came back a few days later, tail between his legs, begging forgiveness. Turns out he didn't want or need to take the other girl out after all. He had just gotten scared. Months later he was down on one knee proposing; now forty-plus years of marriage later, my dad still gazes goopy-eyed at Mom across the dinner table and spouts random poetry at her wonderfulness. Now four decades later, Mom still refers back to that "Gethsemane prayer" as a turning point in her walk with God, when she learned to pour out her pain to God, to beg Him for what she wanted but then humbly submit to His loving care. To trust that even if people made mistakes, God could set things right.

The Line We Shouldn't Cross

Having said all that, here is something to consider as we borrow from the Psalms: There *is* a line that even the angry psalmists don't cross in prayer. They wish horrors on their enemies (keep in mind that Jesus' lesson on forgiving more than seventy times seven times hadn't yet been preached), but never do they turn their anger on God. They *question* God but don't *accuse*. They stop short of pointing the finger.

The psalmists might say, "People are saying *this* about You, God—will You stand by and let them think that? Prove them wrong!" But they *don't* say, "I charge You of wrongdoing, God. I am angry with You; I resent Your decisions and authority; I give up on You." They maintain a respect for God's authority versus their own humanity, acknowledging their own limited perspective and power.

Take David's Psalm 13 as an example, which we explored in the vignette—it opens in the depths but climbs back up to praise:

> *How long, LORD? Will you forget me forever?*
> *How long will you hide your face from me?*
> *How long must I wrestle with my thoughts*
> *and day after day have sorrow in my heart?* . . .

> *But I trust in your unfailing love;*
> *my heart rejoices in your salvation.*
> *I will sing the LORD's praise,*
> *for he has been good to me.*
>
> PSALM 13:1–2, 5–6

This psalm, and many others, can guide our own prayers:

- Teaching us how to view ourselves in light of God's might
- Reminding us that He is God and we are not
- Helping us to find praise in the midst of pain
- Helping us to appreciate who God is and what He has given, even while we beg for relief
- Guiding us in respectfully stating our case before God, confessing the depths of our hurt without pointing a haughty finger
- Showing us how to lament but not complain

In *One Thousand Gifts*, Ann Voskamp beautifully describes the difference between complaint and lament:

> Lament *is a cry of belief in a good God, a God who has His ear to our hearts, a God who transfigures the ugly into beauty.* Complaint *is the bitter howl of unbelief in any benevolent God in this moment, a distrust in the love-beat of the Father's heart. God's anger kindles hot when the essence of the complaint implies doubt in His love. . . . The more I learn His love, the less likely I am to Israelite complain and the more I genuinely lament, complaint that trusts His heart.*[1]

Complaint landed the Israelites in big trouble with God: snakes, plagues, forty years of wandering. But *lament* is a perfectly acceptable cry from a desperate heart. God welcomes our cries, invites our questions, shoulders our fears. But let us guard against the bitter acid of distrust that erodes the heart and disintegrates the relationship; let us resist the resentment that rankles, taking the fragrant incense of prayer and souring it to acrid smoke.

Let's pray like Jesus: honest, respectful, surrendered.

Let's pray like David: open, raw, redeeming pain with praise.

Remember to Thank and Praise

The best way to keep the right posture in prayer, to maintain a spirit of humility and surrender even as we are hurting, is gratitude. A reading of the Psalms uncovers a pattern: many of the most despairing psalms still find a way to praise and thank God from the darkness. (See Psalms 37, 40, 42, and 89 for a few examples.)

When we are sad and frustrated and tired of waiting, how easy it is to forget to thank God. We have to *choose* to praise God for His kindness, generosity, and power. We have to *remember* to thank Him for gifts already given. If you are stuck in your walk with God, waiting for a blessing that won't come, try bringing gratitude and praise back into your prayer life. Surely He has blessed you in the past. Even as you beg God for what you lack, make a point always to end your prayers with gratitude. That simple discipline will transform your perspective: Praise reminds us of His power; gratitude reminds us of His goodness. Together praise and gratitude protect our hearts and restore our hope.

Choose Your Playlist

So what if you have been doing all this—praying, pouring out your soul, praising through pain—but the silence on God's end is still killing you? When we are navigating a waiting season and the journey takes unexpected detours, Satan tries to run his cruel soundtrack in our minds—*God doesn't like you; God is against you; God is not listening*—but God has a soundtrack, too. Maybe it's time to put together a new spiritual playlist.

Let's choose to fill our minds with God's playlist: scriptures and songs that fuel our faith and protect our relationship. God is not silent, as He sometimes seems; He has already given us His Word to tell us how He feels and how He works. It's up to us to use the Bible to fill in God's half of the conversation.

Here are some scriptures on my faith-building playlist:

When I feel . . .	I read. . .
Forgotten or abandoned by God	"Can a mother forget the baby at her breast and have no compassion on the child she has borne? Though she may forget, I will not forget you!" (Isaiah 49:15)
Ignored by God, tired of the wait	Why do you complain, Jacob? Why do you say, Israel, "My way is hidden from the LORD; my cause is disregarded by my God"? Do you not know? Have you not heard? The LORD is the everlasting God, the Creator of the ends of the earth. He will not grow tired or weary, and his understanding no one can fathom. He gives strength to the weary and increases the power of the weak. Even youths grow tired and weary, and young men stumble and fall; but those who hope in the LORD will renew their strength. They will soar on wings like eagles; they will run and not grow weary, they will walk and not be faint. (Isaiah 40:27–31)
Unimportant to God	"Are not two sparrows sold for a penny? Yet not one of them will fall to the ground outside your Father's care. And even the very hairs of your head are all numbered. So don't be afraid; you are worth more than many sparrows." (Matthew 10:29–31)
Disliked by God or insecure in His love	This is love: not that we loved God, but that he loved us and sent his Son as an atoning sacrifice for our sins. . . . And so we know and rely on the love God has for us. God is love. Whoever lives in love lives in God, and God in them. This is how love is made complete among us so that we will have confidence on the day of judgment: In this world we are like Jesus. There is no fear in love. But perfect love drives out fear, because fear has to do with punishment. The one who fears is not made perfect in love. (1 John 4:10, 16–18)
Frustrated by God's slowness	With the Lord a day is like a thousand years, and a thousand years are like a day. The Lord is not slow in keeping his promise, as some understand slowness. Instead he is patient with you, not wanting anyone to perish, but everyone to come to repentance. (2 Peter 3:8–9)

Scriptures like this remind us that when God allows us to wait for something, it doesn't mean He is mad at us. When we are wandering and wondering, David's story and countless other scriptures like these can reset our thinking, protect our trust, and transform our perspective.

Reclaim the Refuge of Prayer

When Satan conspires with fear and insecurity to turn prayer into a battleground, let's fight back. David fought many enemies in his life, but God wasn't one of them. By fighting *alongside* God, not against Him, David enjoyed prayer as a lifelong refuge, a haven where he waited out and waded through the lonely wilderness years. You and I can experience the same.

When the waiting ended and David overcame his enemies and claimed the promised throne, he wrote a song of praise:

> *In my distress I called to the LORD;*
> *I cried to my God for help.*
> *From his temple he heard my voice;*
> *my cry came before him, into his ears. . . .*
> *He rescued me from my powerful enemy,*
> *from my foes, who were too strong for me.*
> *They confronted me in the day of my disaster,*
> *but the LORD was my support.*
> *He brought me out into a spacious place;*
> *he rescued me because he delighted in me.*
> PSALM 18:6, 17–19

Let prayer remain our refuge year after year, however long we wander in the waiting wilderness. Let us never give up on prayer, even when God feels far away. If we run out of words, let us sit and keep company with God, knowing that even in the silence He sees, He hears, and He cares.

Let us borrow words from David and others who have waited and prayed before us.

Let us *keep* praying all of our days.

Let us remember to thank and praise along the way.

And when our waiting season ends, however it ends, let us celebrate with the One who has seen us through, heard us out, and never left our side.

Waiting Room Reading

For Further Study

David's life takes up a lot of biblical real estate, starting in 1 Samuel 16 and going all the way through the end of 2 Samuel. You can also find David's story in 1 Kings 1 and in 1 Chronicles 10–29.

Journal Prompt

Do you need to work through any negative feelings toward God so you can remain close to Him? (Take a look back at the feelings listed on pages 80–81.) What scriptures can fill *your* spiritual playlist, filling in God's half of the conversation? How can you bring gratitude and praise back into your prayer life?

Prayer Prompt

Be merciful to me, LORD, for I am in distress;
  my eyes grow weak with sorrow,
  my soul and body with grief. . . .

But I trust in you, LORD;
  I say, "You are my God."
My times are in your hands.
PSALM 31:9, 14–15

6
Squeaky Wheels
and Little Old Ladies

Jacob's Story
Until You Bless Me

Based on Genesis 32:22–32

Sleep will not come. Every time Jacob shuts his eyes, he sees Esau—red beard, hard eyes, sharp sword—leading four hundred men. Hunting Jacob and his family.

Minutes limp by, every second an age. He sits up, watches the swollen river sluice, shredding the moon's reflection to rippling ribbons. Across the river, through trees at shore's edge, he can just make out a flickering amber smudge—the fire around which his wives and children sleep. He is glad he sent them across the ford ahead of him. Glad of the space alone to think and plan and pray.

Though time feels stalled tonight, tomorrow will come too soon. At the end of it, Jacob will either be reunited with Esau, the brother he swindled twenty years ago—offering apologies, accepting forgiveness, making introductions—or Jacob and his family will all be dead.

Hours earlier the breathless messengers had sprinted into camp, shouting warnings: "Esau is leading a mass of armed men, and they're marching this way!"

Scores of anxious eyes turned on Jacob. The eyes of his wives, his sons, his daughter, his slaves.

Jacob had forced a laugh, loud and confident. "Oh, that's just Esau showing off for his brother. This is his idea of a grand welcoming committee." Everyone had laughed, relieved and excited.

But now, here alone by the water, Jacob's veins ice over with terror.

Four hundred men isn't a welcoming committee. It's an army.

A twig snaps. Suddenly tense, Jacob listens hard. Every muscle coils, ready to spring. For a moment, all he hears is river nudging against the rocky shore.

Snap, snap, crunch.

Jacob leaps to his feet, sword at the ready. "Who's there?"

Into the soft glow of the fire steps a man. Taller than a man should be, broad-shouldered, bristling with golden weapons.

Immediately Jacob knows this is no ordinary man. He has met messengers from the Lord before. They deliver instructions, warnings, and—if you are fortunate—blessings.

Jacob lowers his sword and drops to one knee. "My lord."

The man inclines his head.

"You have a message for me from God?"

The man shakes his head. The firelight plays tricks, keeps his face in the dark, where Jacob cannot read his expression.

Jacob feels a stab of worry. "A warning? About Esau?"

Silence again. A twitch that might be a head shake *no.*

"A blessing, then?"

Still silence. Jacob stands up, bewildered.

The man turns as if to leave, to melt back into the shadows from which he came. "Wait! Don't just leave without words," Jacob says. His thoughts are spinning, plotting. He remembers the famous family story passed down about his grandfather, Abraham—how he fed the messengers of God all those years ago. During that meal, the Lord finally delivered the promise Abraham had been waiting for. Perhaps food would be the way to this angel's heart, too, the way to access his promises.

A plan forms quickly, and Jacob turns on his charming voice, the one that almost always gets him his way. "At least share a meal with me. I have fresh lamb, prepared just this afternoon by my beautiful wife Rachel." He feels his face shine with the familiar wheedling smile. "Please?"

The man takes another step back.

Anger sparks inside, given greater fuel by fear. "*Say something!*"

Jacob demands, louder than he intends. The man's expression seems to darken; the shadows painting his face deepen. Jacob lowers his voice with an effort. "Please." He holds trembling hands out to the man, beseeching. "In a dream the Lord told me to come back home. He promised we'd be safe, but now Esau is bearing down on us. I camped here alone this night to seek God, to seek blessing, to seek safety for my family tomorrow. *I need your blessing!*" The faces of his family flick through his mind: *Rachel, Joseph, Leah, Reuben, Simeon. . .* All needing him, depending on him for protection. What if the Lord had led his family to slaughter? What if God was finally letting Esau take his revenge?

The angel shrugs and turns away. With a roar of desperation, Jacob springs after him and locks his arms around the man's waist. With a grunt, they both fall to the ground. Jacob's chin bangs against the man's elbow; he tastes blood but does not let go.

The man tries to yank free from Jacob's grip. His arms are hard as iron rods. Jacob clings tighter, and he speaks through gritted teeth: "I will not let you go until you bless me." He shifts his grip, tries to wrap his legs around the man's neck.

At last the angel speaks. "I will not," he says, flipping Jacob over onto his back. The air rushes out of Jacob's lungs, leaving him stunned. *Levi, Judah, Dan.* Still gasping, Jacob brings a knee up into the man's gut. The man buckles, and now Jacob is on top.

Naphtali, Gad, Asher. "I can— do this—forever," Jacob pants, grappling to pin the man's arms to the ground. *Issachar, Zebulun, Dinah.* "I don't give up."

Jacob thinks he hears a smile in the man's voice: "And I don't give in." The angel jerks one arm free and smashes an elbow into Jacob's temple. Galaxies wheel across his vision.

"We'll—see—about—that," Jacob grunts.

Stars keep dancing, but Jacob keeps fighting.

Let's be honest: Jacob wasn't exactly a spiritual giant. Far from it, actually. He lied to his father, stole his brother Esau's birthright—oh, and while he was at it, he took his blessing, too—then ran away. Not the kind of stand-up guy you'd expect to become the father of the nation of Israel. But Jacob had one thing going for him: he fought for what he wanted.

Here on the night before the brothers reunite—a meeting that very well may get Jacob killed—Jacob encounters a messenger from God and recognizes an opportunity. In one of the Bible's more bizarre scenes, Jacob grabs the angel, demands a blessing, and refuses to let go until he gets what he wants. All night the men wrestle, locked in battle.

This story has always fascinated me. Honestly? It's weird. But I think God put it in the Bible to tell us some things about Himself and about prayer.

God Calls Us to Persistence in Prayer

God values persistence and perseverance; in fact, He calls us to them. Jacob's perseverance this night earns him a blessing, a name, and a limp (we will come back to the limp later). Time and again, God urges us to persist—in goodness, in hope, and especially in prayer. Take these passages as just a tiny sampling:

> *Let us not become weary in doing good, for at the proper time we will reap a harvest if we do not give up.*
>
> GALATIANS 6:9

> *"Keep asking, and it will be given to you. Keep searching, and you will find. Keep knocking, and the door will be opened to you. For everyone who asks receives, and the one who searches finds, and to the one who knocks, the door will be opened."*
>
> MATTHEW 7:7–8 HCSB

The Bible encourages us not just to "present our requests to God" but to present them repeatedly. Let's take a closer look at Jesus' classic parable about the persistent widow. (I know, you're probably thinking, *I'm reading a book about waiting; Persistent Widow is my middle name.*")

Great storyteller that Jesus was, I imagine Him telling this story with an affectionate smile on His face, maybe pulling off a funny impersonation of a feisty old woman. Who doesn't know a little old lady down the street who just won't give up until she gets her way?

> *Then Jesus told his disciples a parable to show them that they should always pray and not give up. He said: "In a certain town there was a judge who neither feared God nor cared what people thought. And there was a widow in that town who kept coming to him with the plea, 'Grant me justice against my adversary.'*
>
> *"For some time he refused. But finally he said to himself, 'Even though I don't fear God or care what people think, yet because this widow keeps bothering me, I will see that she gets justice, so that she won't eventually come and attack me!'"*
>
> *And the Lord said, "Listen to what the unjust judge says. And will not God bring about justice for his chosen ones, who cry out to him day and night? Will he keep putting them off? I tell you, he will see that they get justice, and quickly."*
>
> Luke 18:1–8

Always pray. Don't give up. The lesson of the parable is clear: God doesn't mind repetitive prayers—in fact, He invites them. But unlike the judge in Jesus' story, our God is not unjust or uncaring; He is a compassionate Father who loves justice and wants to see His children happy. Our persistence proves that we are serious, shows Him what we really want and need.

When I think about this from a parenting perspective, it makes sense. My children make dozens of requests every day, sometimes hundreds, till I feel like a pinball being boinged around kid to kid: "Tie my shoe!"—*ping*—"Where's my toy?"—*ping*—"I need cheese!"—

ping—"I need to *go!*" Many, perhaps most, of those requests are passing whims, not true desires.

When my oldest child was nearly four (and believe me, it still thrills me to be able to write those three beautiful words: *my oldest child*—*my* means she is mine; *oldest* means there's more than one child who belongs to me; *child* is what I prayed to hold all those long nights), she grew obsessed with all things princess. As summer rounded the corner to fall and Christmas began looming in the not-so-distant future, she fixated on only one Christmas request: the pink dress that Ariel wears when she first becomes human in *The Little Mermaid*. You don't remember that dress, you say? Neither does anyone else, since Ariel only wears the dress for seventy-three seconds in the film. But my beloved daughter wanted one, so off I set, searching the world for the pink dress. It didn't exist.

At first I tried the old Distraction Technique, showing Cassidy picture after picture of other princess dresses: "Don't you love Cinderella's blue dress? No? *Ooh la!* Look at this yellow Belle dress! With *ruffles*! No? Oh, look at this *amaaaaazing* wedding-y Ariel dress! Isn't that even more gorgeous than the pink dress?" But Cassidy stood firm. Didn't even bat an eye at the other unworthy imitations.

So I tried the old Give-It-Time Technique. Surely she would forget about the dress after a while, move on to something else. She was four! How long could her attention span be? But as December descended, bringing cold and Christmas trees, Cassidy insisted: the pink dress.

Still the pink dress.

Only the pink dress.

Exactly as it looked in the film.

After so many months of her unflagging refrain, I gave in, finally convinced. The pink dress really was her heart's desire. I had to find a way.

So I conscripted a seamstress friend to design and sew the world's first pink Ariel princess dress. Come Christmas morning, Cassidy was all swirling pink skirts, all little-girl glee. I had never seen her happier. Her persistence had paid off.

I suspect our interactions with God in prayer sometimes work like this. He is not withholding gifts just to be stingy or mean—He is just giving us time to search our hearts and discover our true desires.

Are you beginning to feel stupid asking God for the same thing over and over, day after day, for months or years on end? Don't. Are you wondering if God thinks you are being annoying or pushy or selfish? He doesn't. It's not wrong to be the squeaky wheel, the persistent widow who keeps asking. Remember: *God encouraged us to do it!*

Sometimes God Changes His Mind

It would have been easy for Cassidy to give up on her dress, to let me talk her out of it. But she didn't. She knew what she wanted.

It would have been easy for Jacob to give up the fight, admit he was outmatched. But he didn't. He knew what he needed.

Sometimes when we've been waiting for a long time, we give up on praying because we think, *God has already decided what's going to happen, so why should I bother telling Him what I want? He is just going to do what He wants anyway.*

Not necessarily.

Ready to take a deeper doctrinal dive? Hold your breath. . .

In chapter 1, I hinted at a theological mind bender. When we pray, we usually expect one of three answers from God: *yes, no,* or *wait.* But I suggest that He offers a fourth response: *Maybe. Ask Me again; you might talk Me into it.*

Consider Jacob's grandfather, Abraham, known as the "father of the faithful." In Genesis 18:20 we find that the city of Sodom has become a sin-saturated blight, and God has decided to destroy it. The decision has been made, the demolition date already set. It's a done deal. *But Abraham convinces God to reconsider.* At first, Abraham's request is tentative: "Will you really sweep it away and not spare the place for the sake of the fifty righteous people in it? Far be it from you to do such a thing. . . . Will not the Judge of all the earth do right?" (verses 24–25).

I suspect Abraham cringes here, waiting for God's answer, wondering if he has crossed the line, made God angry. But you know what? *God listens to Abraham!* He changes His plan and agrees to spare the city if fifty righteous people can be found.

But Abraham isn't done bargaining. He says, "Now that I have been so bold as to speak to the Lord, though I am nothing but dust and ashes, what if the number of the righteous is five less than fifty?" (verses 27–28). Again God agrees.

From forty-five people, to forty, to thirty, to twenty, all the way down to ten, Abraham humbly talks God down, persuading Him to spare the city of Sodom if He can find just ten righteous souls there. God originally had a different plan, but Abraham convinces Him to reconsider, to change. (In the end, God still destroyed Sodom—He was *willing* to spare it but could not find even ten righteous people in the entire city.)

And Abraham wasn't the only one who talked God into changing His plan. Take a look at King Hezekiah, whose story appears in Isaiah 38:

> *In those days Hezekiah became ill and was at the point of death. The prophet Isaiah son of Amoz went to him and said, "This is what the LORD says: Put your house in order, because you are going to die; you will not recover."*
>
> *Hezekiah turned his face to the wall and prayed to the LORD, "Remember, LORD, how I have walked before you faithfully and with wholehearted devotion and have done what is good in your eyes." And Hezekiah wept bitterly.*
>
> *Then the word of the LORD came to Isaiah: "Go and tell Hezekiah, 'This is what the LORD, the God of your father David, says:* I have heard your prayer and seen your tears; *I will add fifteen years to your life.'"*
>
> VERSES 1–5, emphasis added

What a story! God had decided that Hezekiah's time had come, and yet Hezekiah's prayer changed God's mind and Hezekiah's fate.

What does this tell us? Our prayers make a difference.

I have heard your prayer and seen your tears. So much love, in such simple words. Just as we saw in Exodus 3:7, God sees, God hears, God cares.

God, compassionate Father, sometimes changes His plans just because we, beloved children, ask Him to.

Lessons from Jesus' Prayer Life: Have the Conversation

I'm not suggesting we will always get what we ask for, what we are waiting for. We won't. Sometimes we wait forever, ask ten thousand times, and in the end we still get a *no*. (And even when we *do* get The Thing, it almost always comes to us differently than the way we had envisioned.)

Take God's very own Son as an example. Let's step into another nighttime wrestling match: Jesus in the garden of Gethsemane, the night of His arrest.

Jesus knows the Father has firmly decided on a plan for saving mankind, and that plan involves Jesus' suffering and death. God has spent generations preparing the way, setting the stage: messianic prophecies, a complex family tree in frequent need of dramatic rescue (crazy plagues, parted seas, unlikely heroes), a virgin birth, a midnight escape to Egypt. . . We are talking massive strategizing that spanned millennia and affected millions. After all this effort, the cross is to be God's crowning achievement, the consummate expression of His love for mankind.

At last the stage is set. The actors, all in place. The curtain, already rising. Jesus knows all this. He has spent years, a lifetime, preparing Himself for this night, this sacrifice. . .but here in the final moments, *Jesus asks God to change His mind.* He pleads, "My Father, if it is possible, may this cup be taken from me."

Jesus knows God probably won't say yes—*can't* say yes, however much He may want to—but even so, *Jesus has the conversation.*

Jesus knows God more intimately than any of us ever will. The fact that Jesus asks God to change His mind, even in the final hours, tells us a lot about God:

God is approachable. He invites our honest thoughts and will consider our requests, even when they stand at odds with His plans.

God is flexible. Jesus understood that God is flexible, open to considering our desires as He makes His plans. Sometimes, as we have seen with Abraham and Hezekiah, God can be convinced to alter His initial plan. In Jesus' case, God didn't change His mind, but He did go out of His way to comfort His Son, even sending an angel to strengthen Jesus as He prayed.

These stories give me hope and fuel my prayers. They convince me that our prayers matter—yes, even the repetitive, squeaky-wheel requests we think God is sick of hearing. These stories renew my faith in prayer's "appeal process." Prayer is no one-way conversation, however much it may sometimes feel that way. Our relationship with God involves give-and-take, and He cares about our opinions. God weighs our desires in light of His plans and our best interests, and sometimes He gives us what we want *because we asked.* Because He cares.

We Get a Say

I have seen all these principles of perseverance at work during my own waiting seasons. I started pursuing a writing career when I was twenty-six, smack in the middle of our ongoing struggle to get pregnant. At first, things moved fast. I wrote my first novel, *The Thirteenth Summer*, in nine and a half months. (How clever, I thought, that even though I couldn't get pregnant at the time, birthing my first "book baby" took the exact same amount of time as growing a human baby!) I went to a writer's conference, studied the industry, revised my work, sent queries to seven literary agents, and *bam*! In a remarkably short time, I had signed with a fabulous literary agent who started shopping my work around to Big New York Book People. *This is happening!* I thought. *I don't know why everybody says it's so hard to make it as a writer! I see what God is doing: He delayed me getting pregnant because He wanted to give me time to become a famous novelist!*

Womp womp.

So much for my reading-God's-mind ability. Turns out I was in for a lot of heartbreak and disappointment, for more rejections and years of working and waiting than my twenty-six-year-old brain could have possibly fathomed. If you had told me that first year that I would still be waiting for a career break in three years, I would have swallowed hard. Five years—I would have gone misty-eyed. Ten years—I would have tossed my laptop out the window. Thirteen years—I would have kung-fu'd you in the face.

But let's check in at the ten-years-waiting point.

Now thirty-six, I was crying in my parents' living room, venting to my entire extended family, throwing a full-on pity party, probably terrifying my new brother-in-law. I cried about how all my friends were at the point in their careers where they were "making it," but here I was, stuck at square one, now without even a literary agent to represent my work. How I was beginning to wonder if God even wanted me to write. If I'd wasted ten years of my life on an idiotic dream. If the ten years of working and waiting were God's not-so-subtle way of saying, *"The answer is no, Elizabeth. A writing career isn't My will for you. Get a different dream."*

My family disagreed. They urged me to be careful not to get all "Christian superstitious," attempting to interpret God's opinions based on life events. (See chapter 4 for a more thorough discussion of the dangers of trying to read God's mind.)

It took two more long years of praying and writing, doubting and fighting, before I signed with a new agent. And then it took yet another year and a half before I got a book deal—but not in teen fiction, where I started out. My first book deal? Yep, you guessed it: for a Christian book called *When God Says, "Wait."*

Let's just pause so you can put down your book and properly laugh your head off at me—and marvel at God's sense of irony.

I didn't set out to write Christian books or nonfiction books or books for grown-ups. But through a winding, thirteen-year journey and ten thousand prayers, God pointed me here, to the words I'm typing even now. Prepared me to write this book, which I couldn't have written without those thirteen miserable years. My desires informed God's decisions, and in time He directed me to where He wanted me.

We have seen how even Jesus was not spared drinking the cup of suffering God had set out for Him. Jesus asked, but God said no. We don't know what God has planned for our lives—will you get that promotion, that engagement ring, that healing?—because only God can answer for sure. But we do know that God welcomes our prayers—the repetitive, the heartbroken, the passionate—and He hears them. Though we are "but dust and ashes" (Genesis 18:27), our words matter. Our feelings matter. God takes our desires into account.

Isaiah 55:8–9 tells us God's ways are higher than our ways, His thoughts higher than our thoughts. Although we can't fully comprehend the complex relationship between God's will, God's plans, and our desires, the Bible does indicate, in a thousand different ways, that *we get a say*. Our desires inform God's decisions. He considers our feelings. God cares about our perspective, our free will, and our happiness. He wanted to hear Jesus' thoughts, Abraham's thoughts, Hezekiah's thoughts, Jacob's thoughts—and He wants to hear ours. Yours and mine. We are not silent pawns in a celestial chess match, being moved around and sacrificed for the sake of God's big-picture strategy. There is a conversation, a relationship, a give-and-take.

The Price of a Wrestling Match

Let's revisit Jacob's angelic encounter. All night they wrestle, man and God, and still Jacob won't let go. Dawn breaks. Finally, the messenger gives in and gives Jacob his blessing, but Jacob is not left untouched. The angel dislocates Jacob's hip. The Hebrew word for *dislocates* can also mean *makes lame*, so it's possible that for the rest of his life Jacob would walk with a limp. He receives a blessing, but the battle leaves a scar. Jacob is never quite the same: greatly blessed, forever changed. He even gets a new name: instead of *Jacob* (meaning "he grabs the heel" or "he deceives"), he becomes *Israel* (most likely meaning "he struggles with God").

Every waiting season in my life has left its mark on me. I have memories, scars. And honestly? I don't mind the scars anymore. They are part of me now; I wouldn't recognize myself without them. They make me who I am: The girl who loved a boy who didn't love her back. The girl who couldn't get pregnant. The girl who couldn't get a book deal.

The girl whose future hangs trembling, uncertain, even now, as her husband considers a job change and a big move. She stands in the fork, straining to see. Nearsighted, frustrated. With two diverging paths—different futures, different lives—beckoning. Two places, two peoples, she loves.

Some of those questions have been resolved—some *waits* turned into *yeses*, some into *nos*—but I am still that girl, still all of those girls. Different now, but still with the memories. Still with the scars. I have my wounds from waiting; you have yours.

The rest of Jacob's life is defined as before and after this night. Before this prayer, he is Jacob. After, he is Israel. Another man entirely. Whatever you are waiting for right now, you may one day divide your life into before and after this season, these prayers.

I can't tell you how this season of waiting will end, but end it will. Let's take a lesson from an unlikely teacher, Jacob: if there are blessings we want or things we need, let's ask boldly, persistently.

When battles change us, even wound us, we can use our scars for good: They are reminders of God's power in our weakness. Memories of His care and concern. Marks that help us encourage friends in their sufferings: *I've been down in that dirt. It gets better from here.*

Let's wrestle in prayer. Roll in the dirt. Grapple and bleed. Whatever God's final answer, we will be stronger for the struggle.

Waiting Room Reading

For Further Study
Read Jacob's life story (and the story of his children) in Genesis 25–35, 37–50.

Journal Prompt
Do you view God as being flexible and approachable? Do you think He *wants* to hear your persistent prayers, or do you secretly suspect

you are annoying Him? What scars has waiting given you? For better or worse, how have your waiting seasons already changed you?

Prayer Prompt

Relent, Lord! How long will it be?
Have compassion on your servants.
Satisfy us in the morning with your unfailing love,
that we may sing for joy and be glad all our days.
Make us glad for as many days as you have afflicted us,
for as many years as we have seen trouble.
May your deeds be shown to your servants,
your splendor to their children.

May the favor of the Lord our God rest on us;
establish the work of our hands for us—
yes, establish the work of our hands.
Psalm 90:13–17

7
The Friends Who See You Through

Ruth's Story
The Longest Day

Based on Ruth 3 and 4

Ruth eases the door open and tiptoes inside the tiny house she shares with her mother-in-law. Removing her sandals, she reaches for the water jug. She should be exhausted after the night she has had, but her heart is thrumming, her mind turning cartwheels.

"Well?" a throaty voice calls out from the darkness.

Ruth whirls around, brandishing the jug like a sword.

Her mother-in-law cackles from her chair in the corner. A candle yawns to life, stretches toward the ceiling, revealing Naomi—*Mara*, Ruth corrects herself, for the ten thousandth time—blanket-wrapped in her chair. Waiting for dawn, waiting for Ruth, and grinning. "I don't know what you planned to do with that jug, but if I were a thief, I'd think twice before breaking in!"

Ruth feels her own laughter bubbling up to meet Mara's—how long has it been since she has heard Mara's raspy laugh? She finds her humor tangling with tears. Ruth's dead husband, Mahlon, used to get his mother laughing so hard her lungs would protest, till they all feared Naomi—she was *Naomi* then, *Pleasant*—might laugh herself to death. But her laughter had died with her sons, and she had buried her smile with her husband. Only in recent months had the smile resurrected.

"Pity the thief who defies the wrath of my pitcher," Ruth says, waving the jug around. "But, Mother,"—she bends a disapproving look on Mara—"you shouldn't have waited up all night."

Clucking in disagreement, Mara heaves herself to her feet. The candlelight sparkles in her eyes, along with—is it hope Ruth sees shining there?

"Well?" Mara's voice rings eager. "How did it go, daughter—your night at Boaz's feet? Will he redeem our family property? Will he take you for his bride?"

"I—I think so." Careful words, calm voice. Life has taught Ruth not to hope too hard or too soon. "Just as you said, he woke in the night and found me there at his feet." Warmth kindles in her cheeks. "He said if our kinsman-redeemer does not want to redeem, then he—Boaz—will do it himself." Wrestling with a sudden shyness, Ruth ends on a whisper.

Feeling Mara's eyes studying her, Ruth ducks her head and reaches for her shawl, unknotting it on the battered wooden table. "Look, Mother—he wouldn't let me come back empty-handed, so he gave me all this barley." A smile plays around her mouth. "He is—very kind."

Mara's wrinkled hand catches Ruth's elbow. "Mark my words: Boaz will not rest until the matter is settled." She squeezes so tight Ruth bites back a squeak of pain. "Just wait, daughter. By tonight I will have found you a husband." She flashes an impish grin. "And what a husband Boaz will make! Wealthy, influential, and—he is gray but still handsome, is he not?"

"Mother!" Ruth swats at Mara's shoulder with the corner of her shawl. Cackling, Mara limps back to her chair.

Hours crawl by. Ruth starts in on the barley—some for bread, some for stew, some for storage. When that doesn't fill enough time, she starts cleaning things that don't need cleaning. In her corner, Mara's fingers fly over the mending, but today she hums quietly.

The humming is new. Actually old—a long-lost habit from happier days. It wakes something in Ruth till she can hardly think, hardly breathe.

Just before dusk, fists pound on the door. Muffled voices call: "Ruth! Nao—*Mara*! Let us in! We have news!"

Eyes meet.

Time stops.

Mara's crinkled eyes reflect Ruth's own hectic feelings: *This is it.*

Ruth opens the door. Two old women barrel in, flattening Ruth against the table.

"Took you long enough," says Rachel.

"Like to catch our death," harrumphs Anna, a tease in her voice.

And then their words coil, overlapping, interrupting, and Ruth struggles to follow the looping thoughts: "Such news—She won't believe, will she, sister?—No, not in her wildest—"

"Aaron just came from the city gate. Everyone is talking—"

Ruth feels Mara's hand slip around hers and give a hard squeeze.

"Aaron couldn't believe it himself—"

"Oh, yes, sister, he did seem shocked—"

"*What's the news?*" Mara's voice thunders over the chaos, and for two seconds the sisters fall silent, jaws hanging open.

"Well, I never," huffs Rachel.

Anna jumps back in, head bobbing. "The nerve, talking to old friends—"

"Cousins, sister, we are cousins—"

Mara stomps her foot. "You're doing it again!" She draws a deep breath, mouth twitching. "Rachel, dear, please just tell us the news. *By yourself.*"

Anna glowers. Folds her arms across her ample bosom. Presses her lips together. Ruth fights a laugh.

Chest puffing up, Rachel rattles off a string of words: "Boaz has redeemed your family's property! He offered it to Nathan, the nearer relative, but Nathan could not do it, so Boaz has stepped in. The deal is already done!" Rachel turns glowing eyes on Ruth. "And you, my dear, will be—"

"His bride!" Anna's voice joins in, high-pitched and squeaky. The sisters clutch each other in a sideways hug, beaming.

"Oh, my daughter," Mara breathes, clasping Ruth's wrists. Ruth turns to face her, and joy—true joy, unguarded—radiates from her mother-in-law's face.

The old promise echoes between them: "*Your people, my people; your God, my God.*"

"To see you a bride again—this has long been my prayer." Mara's eyes glisten. "My Mahlon, he would want this. To see you happy, to see you settled, to see you"—she pauses, a heartbeat—"a mother at last."

Ruth forces words past crowded memories, all caught in her throat. "You are sure? He would not—resent this?"

"No, child." Mara presses a cool palm against Ruth's cheek; Ruth leans into it. "Mahlon would rejoice. He loved you enough to let you go. To wish for your happiness, even if"—she gives a brave and trembling smile—"even after he was gone. If he could not grow old with you, he would be proud to see a man like Boaz step in."

Ruth's tears spill, relief and surprise and sorrow and memory and happiness—happiness, she had forgotten the feeling—all mingled, raining down.

Behind Mara, a loud honking sound: Anna, blowing her nose in her sister's shawl, both sisters streaming tears, gazing dreamy-eyed at Ruth. "Oh, sister," Anna starts, "she will make the most beautiful bride—"

Now Rachel: "Oh yes, the most beautiful—wait, except my Hadassah—"

"Oh yes, except your Hadassah—but second-most-beautiful to our Hadassah, and the whole village will—"

Suddenly Mara is laughing, head thrown back, wheezing, and Ruth is laughing, and the sisters are laughing, and Ruth is caught up in a sister squish, hugged by more arms than she can count.

And Mara—Mara starts bouncing, up and down, a little girl with young knees, starry eyes, open heart. "A wedding, we're going to have a wedding!"

"And *babies*!" shouts Anna. "Lots and lots of grandbabies for Mara!"

"Twins!" says Rachel.

"Just one will do," Mara winks, locking shining eyes on Ruth. "I can't wait."

Ruth and Naomi waited long to find healing and happiness after profound loss. If they hadn't clung to each other, I wonder what would have happened to them—two widows, one young, one aging, flung on the mercies of Naomi's old hometown, in an era when women could not provide for themselves. With God's help, Ruth and Naomi healed each other. Kept each other company on the long husbandless nights. Took turns mourning, weeping, remembering. Worked together to carve out a life and claim a home.

Ruth stepped in as Naomi's daughter. She followed Naomi to Israel instead of returning to her own family. *"Your people, my people; your God, my God."* After a time, Naomi returned the favor, finding Ruth a husband, a home, and happiness. In turn, Ruth gave Naomi the grandson she never thought she would hold, helping her reclaim the joyful spirit she had lost. When friends speak of Naomi at the end of her life, they no longer call her Mara ("bitter"); they once more call her Naomi ("pleasant"). "Naomi," they exclaim, "has a son!" (Ruth 4:17).

You never forget the people who wait with you, the friends who pray for you and with you. Who put up with you and your moods. Who listen to your rants, and still like you at the end of them. Who gently turn you back to God when you have turned the wrong way. Who still see the best in you even after you have revealed your worst.

Alexandra, Emma, Sara, Mindi, Julie, Melissa, Laura, Karen, Heather, Allison, Nina, Katie, Mary, Kimberly, Susan, Elva, Carmen, Tammica—these are just a few of the women who have waited and prayed with me, and I with them, during bleak waiting seasons. Though distance means I rarely see some of them in person, we share forever bonds.

The Friendship Ideal

Devoted friendship ran strong in Naomi's family. Three generations later, the Bible offers us another epic relationship: Israel's first king, Saul, has a son. Saul's son, Jonathan, befriends Ruth's great-grandson,

David. Jonathan is next in line for Israel's throne, but when David—upstart shepherd, giant-slayer, singer-songwriter—slingshots his way onto the scene, Jonathan loves him. Gives him his heart and gives him his sword. Their relationship is a remarkable model of friendship, the kind we all long to find.

My favorite aspects of their friendship? The selflessness, sacrifice, and spirituality:

> *While David was at Horesh in the Desert of Ziph, he learned that Saul had come out to take his life. And Saul's son Jonathan went to David at Horesh and helped him find strength in God. "Don't be afraid," he said. "My father Saul will not lay a hand on you. You will be king over Israel, and I will be second to you. Even my father Saul knows this." The two of them made a covenant before the LORD. Then Jonathan went home, but David remained at Horesh.*
>
> 1 SAMUEL 23:15–18

Selflessness, sacrifice, and spirituality are things you and I can bring into *any* friendship. While we can't expect every friendship to be as close-knit as David and Jonathan's—in my observation, kindred-spirit, *I-will-die-for-you* friendships like this come along only a few times in life, maybe only once or twice—we can still be Jonathans and Davids to friends in need.

We can help one another find strength in God. We can pray together, point each other to scripture, and remind each other of God's promises. We can comfort each other, listen to each other, and just as Jonathan did for David at Horeb, we can simply show up and keep watch.

The Friendship Myth

Let's take a time-out here for a second. Waiting can be intensely lonely. You feel like all your peers are moving forward—finding success, experiencing joy—while there you sit, stuck in neutral, or worse, reverse. At a time when we need friends more than ever, it's tempting to withdraw into our own struggle, convinced that no one relates, no one understands, no one cares. The longer we wait, the lonelier we may feel.

So friendship can be a tender topic. But let's talk about it anyway—gently, gently. ("Gentlyyyyy!" Random *Princess Bride* quote, anyone? Anyway.) First, let's deal with the Friendship Myth.

What's the Friendship Myth? *Everyone else has closer friends than I have.*

We look around, and we are sure everyone else has *I'd-gladly-give-you-my-kidney*-level BFFs. Social media certainly makes it look that way, because of course no one posts pictures of "that time I hurt her feelings and we acted weird for two months" or "that time she talked about herself for three hours and forgot to ask me how I was doing." No, all the pictures show people beaming cheek to cheek, looking like they have never argued, never hurt each other, never let each other down. Well, remember this: for every picture that paints a thousand words, the next one leaves out ten thousand! Friendships are wonderful, but they're complicated and messy, too. They are up and down, and they go through phases. But you know what? They are totally have-able, even while we are waiting.

After a lot of angst over the years, here are a few things I've learned about the insecurities-about-friendships issue:

Every friendship is different. We can't force friends into a one-size-fits-all relationship. We can't compare or rank friendships. Your friendships are *yours*, and they might look and feel different than other people's—different from David and Jonathan's, and Ruth and Naomi's—but that doesn't make them less valuable, less meaningful, or less real.

Celebrate each other's quirks. The most satisfying friendships are the ones where we let each other be ourselves. We embrace and enjoy each other, quirks, flaws, and all. We give a lot of grace. We call each other higher spiritually, we seek to grow together, and we are honest, but we also respect our differences and allow each other space and time to mature.

Be the friend you wish you had, no strings attached. I have found that if I go into friendships with expectations, I get disappointed and hurt. The other person rarely meets my unspoken hopes. But if I go into a friendship to give, it's amazing how much I get back. Selflessness is a biblical principle: "Give, and it will be given to you. A good measure, pressed down, shaken together and running over, will be poured into your lap. For with the measure you use, it will be measured to you" (Luke 6:38). This principle is also reflected in the Golden Rule: "Do to others what you would have them do to you" (Matthew 7:12).

Some friends come into our lives for only a season. Some friendships come into our lives so that we can minister to each other for a time. This is especially true during waiting seasons, when we may connect with others suffering a similar health crisis or heartache. We comfort and support each other for a time, and when that time ends, our affection and memories remain, but our day-to-day time and attention may focus elsewhere. And *that's okay*. It doesn't mean the friendship was insincere; it just means that life sometimes takes us other places.

Friendship with God

Let's backtrack a little from all this talk about people to talk about friendship with God. People can never occupy the God-shaped space in our hearts, no matter how thoughtful or devoted or almost-perfect they are. When we try to get people (even siblings or parents or best friends for life or even the love of our life) to become our *everything*, they will always fall short. We will still be left lonely. Why? Because only God is meant to be our everything.

I have always appreciated Proverbs 14:10: "Each heart knows its own bitterness, and no one else can share its joy." Some feelings are too intense to express, impossible to explain. We long to share, to be understood, but words fail.

No one else can fully understand all we feel—no one, that is, but God. When we are grieving, no one but God can fully feel our pain. When we are so singing-in-the-rain happy that we think our heart may explode, no one but God can fully feel our joy. God alone can hear our inmost thoughts; the Holy Spirit communicates our deepest desires to Him:

> *The Spirit helps us in our weakness. We do not know what we ought to pray for, but the Spirit himself intercedes for us through wordless groans. And he who searches our hearts knows the mind of the Spirit, because the Spirit intercedes for God's people in accordance with the will of God.*
>
> ROMANS 8:26–27

I have noticed something in myself these past few years: I have been tempted to seek comfort, celebration, and commiseration from social media instead of from *God*. Something bad happens, and my first thought isn't *Let me pray about this*, but *Let me post about this*. Something good happens, something exciting, something funny. . .and prayer isn't always my first outlet. It's not wrong to share our lives with friends online—social media can provide powerful support—but if God is not *first* meeting our emotional needs, then social media will leave us feeling unsatisfied and vaguely lonely.

Want to feel closer to God emotionally?

Post less, pray more. Pray first, post last.

Share with God your grief, your joy, and everything in between. Let Him carry the lion's share of your emotions. Peter urges us, "Cast all your anxiety on him because he cares for you" (1 Peter 5:7). *All* means *all*! Let's take God up on that promise. (See chapters 5 and 6 for a full exploration of our prayer life during waiting seasons.)

Relationships at Risk: Protecting Your "Go-To" Relationship

As much as we don't want it to—as much as we want to pretend that everything is fine—waiting affects our relationships. As time wore on during our years of baby-waiting, my ever-deepening sadness began to wear on Kevin. He wanted a baby, too, but of course it was different for him—partly because he is a man and partly because he is a naturally joyful, faithful person. He desperately wanted to make me happy—to "fix" the problem—but he couldn't. As I changed, my happy husband changed, too. His cheerful whistling around the house quieted; his silly jokes grew sparse. When I realized what was happening, I vowed I would not let my sadness destroy the man I loved or the marriage I had spent so many years praying for God to give me.

People who love us will gladly offer a sympathetic ear and a shoulder to cry on as often as they can, but even so, everyone has limits. Our "go-to" person (whether friend, mother, sister, boyfriend, or husband) may not be available every time we need to talk; one single person can't carry our entire burden, however much he or she may want to.

How can we protect our go-to relationship?

Go to God first. Go to God before you go to your go-to person!

Remember, relationships go two ways. We can't expect a one-way relationship in which someone constantly asks how we are, listens to all our woes, and offers us support. Our person has struggles and fears, too; our person is waiting for things, too. My friend Emma and I seem to take turns calling each other midcrisis, hiding from children in closets and laundry rooms so we can spill out our woes in private. (We are usually interrupted by some small person shouting, "Mommy! Are you in there? If you don't find my sock right now, I will die!" But still we try to listen—to take turns being the one to hurt, the one to comfort—and somehow it works. We both hang up happier.)

Change the subject. Even though you know and I know that The Thing is the *only thing* on our mind almost all the time, our go-to person needs to talk about other things. And honestly? It's good for us to change the subject in our own minds every once in a while! It's good for us to give.

Say thank you. When we are waiting, we may feel cheated out of something we feel we deserve. Somehow, that can make us feel entitled to special attention and service from our go-to person, and chances are, he or she is happy to offer it. But let's be careful. Let's go out of our way to express love, affection, gratitude, and encourage-ment to friends and family who wait with us, realizing their devotion is a gift, not an obligation. A little thanks goes a long way.

Accept imperfect understanding. People—even the people who love us most—will not fully understand every nuance of what we feel while we are waiting. *That's okay.* Perfect understanding is God's job, not a person's job.

Don't expect mind reading. When we are feeling especially down or needy, it's not fair to expect people to read our minds, and then get angry when they miss our cues. We have to *tell* people what we feel and what we need!

Be generous in return. The time will come when it's your turn to give back. When that day comes, give as it has been given to you!

Share the load among several people. And that leads us to our next point. . .

Open Your Heart to New People

Waiting seasons have taught me to expand my support system. Even though some struggles may feel more private than others, I encourage you to take a risk. Let new people in. Open your heart to a few more confidants. You will be surprised by how many people love you enough to want to shoulder a part of your burden. I am forever grateful to the precious friends who have prayed and fasted with and for me, listened to me, and sat and cried with me during times of need. They have preserved my sanity, my walk with God, and even my marriage.

So how do we build new and meaningful friendships?

Look around. When we are lonely, we might wish a new friend would just fall from the sky or move in next door. Once in a while someone new shows up, but chances are, you already have some great candidates for friendship in your life right now—at church, at work, in your neighborhood. Ask God to open your eyes and guide you.

Take risks. If we will take small risks—asking someone to meet for coffee, opening up about our lives, inviting friendship—we will create opportunities. I met Emma—Emma of the hiding-and-crying-in-closets-and-laundry-room phone calls—in a Barnes & Noble bathroom. (This is strangely appropriate.) We started chatting by the sinks because we had daughters the same age. Emma put herself out there and said, "Hey, can we be friends? None of my friends has a child my daughter's age!" We swapped numbers—a toilet flushed, as if to signal the significance of the moment—and just like that, one of the most important friendships of both our lives, and our daughters' lives, was born.

Break the ice. How do you start opening up to new people if you aren't used to it? It's not as complicated as we make it. We open our hearts by opening our mouths. Share a detail or two and see what happens. The worst you will get is a blank stare or an insensitive comment. I once mentioned our miscarriage to a new friend, and her panic and discomfort were almost palpable. I have never seen anyone work so hard to change the subject so fast. I immediately realized we would be playdate friends, not heart-to-heart friends, and that was fine. But most of the time, openness prompts empathy and reciprocation.

Look outside the box. If you can't find local friends or family to shoulder your burden, look into some alternate options. A dear friend of mine received wonderful encouragement from an online support group during a time of loss in her life. None of her in-town friends could relate to her struggle at the time, but she found a creative way to fill the void.

Relationships at Risk: The Pitfall of Envy

So let's say you are waiting, and you have some decent friendships. What a great blessing! But. . .*but.* By now you have probably already realized that Satan would love to use waiting times to destroy not only your faith and joy but your friendships as well.

My redheaded friend left her life, her friends, and her home and took a new job in her boyfriend's city, visions of wedding rings dancing in her head. She already had her bridal party tentatively picked out, including a close friend from back home who was also in a serious dating relationship. But two weeks after the Redhead moved, in a devastating turn of events, she broke up with The Boy. It's not the kind of thing you post on Facebook, so the news spread slowly.

Five days after the breakup, Redhead gets a phone call from the former potential bridesmaid:

> Redhead: (*Picks up, thinking the friend must have heard the news, must be calling to console her.*) Hello?
> Former Potential Bridesmaid for the Wedding That Will Never Happen: Hi! How's the new city? (*Doesn't pause long enough to let Redhead summon energy to explain. Starts talking again at hyperspeed.*) So I have news! (*Dramatic pause in which Redhead's heart sinks, already knowing.*) I'm engaged!
> Redhead: (*Manages to make a happy sound.*) Congratulations!
> Former Potential Bridesmaid: (*Talks without stopping, rattling off the engagement story, as Redhead drips silent tears on the other end. Twenty minutes later. . .*) So? How are things with The Boy? Think he'll propose soon?
> Redhead: Uh, so. . .we broke up.
> *Shocked silence.*

For the next ten minutes, they fumble around—Engaged Girl apologizes and offers appropriate sympathy, Redhead tries not to cry her eyeballs out. The conversation is infinitely awkward, exceptionally painful. Their lives have taken sharp turns in different directions, and neither knows how to navigate the space between.

That was five years ago. They have not spoken since.

Neither of them did anything wrong, neither of them wanted to hurt the other, but they just couldn't figure it out. Couldn't bridge the divide. What do you do when one of you is happy, the other still waiting?

I feel their pain. This lovely scene happened smack in the middle of my couldn't-get-pregnant years:

> Me (*answering very large pre-iPhone flip phone*): Hello?
> Lifelong Friend (*breathless and happy*): You'll never guess what happened!

Me: Um. . .I forgot to call on your eight-month wedding anniversary?

Her: No! I'm pregnant! *On the pill!* How does that even happen?

Me: (*Eight seconds of stunned silence, waging war with a truckload of chaotic and sinful thoughts. Summoning Academy Award-level acting skills, forcing joy into my voice.*) Um, congratulations!

Her: Thanks! I know this is hard for. . .oh, shoot. . .*bleaar-ghhhhh* [that's how you spell "vomits violently"]. Hey, I gotta go. I can't (*more vomit sounds*)—Bye.

Me: (*Eight hours of weeping.*)

I wrestled with resentment toward God and envy of my friend. I knew that if I didn't overcome these temptations, I might ruin our friendship. I would pull back and put distance between us, my jealousy would hurt her, and our thirteen-year friendship might never recover.

We made it through the long-distance pregnancy, but then the baby was born.

Before she brought her son to visit me, I spent weeks preparing my heart. I stumbled across this scripture, which is found in a completely different context, but whose spirit applied perfectly to what I was facing:

> *They came to John and said to him, "Rabbi, that man who was with you on the other side of the Jordan—the one you testified about—look, he is baptizing, and everyone is going to him."*
>
> *To this John replied, "A person can receive* only what is given them from heaven.*"*
>
> JOHN 3:26–27, emphasis added

John chose not to envy Jesus' ministry success; he trusted that God was giving each of them the work He wanted them to do. Like John, I knew I had to choose to rejoice in the gift God had given my friend, even though the timing made no sense to me. My friend hadn't done anything wrong—she hadn't gotten pregnant on purpose to rub my infertility in my face!—but God in His wisdom had given her a child, and as almighty God, He had the right to do so. With those things in mind, I prepared my heart. God gave me the strength to overcome temptation, and we had a wonderful weekend together. I found true joy in holding her son, playing with him, and watching her embrace her new role as a mother.

That weekend was a key victory for me. God helped me conquer what could have been a friendship-ending temptation, and the memory of that victory served me well in future struggles.

Don't let envy alienate precious friendships. Let's pray to "rejoice with those who rejoice," just as we hope friends will mourn with us (Romans 12:15). Our turn for joy will come one way or another, and when that day comes, we still want to have friends left to celebrate with us!

While we are waiting, our friends may get jobs, get engaged, or get pregnant. That's okay. Our friendship can survive the challenge. Our friends might even get lost in their own happiness for a while, less sensitive to our heartache than they used to be (or maybe they are just uncertain of how to navigate the awkwardness). That's okay, too. If we will give grace—the kind of grace they sometimes show us—the friendship can survive.

But here's a thought: In the interest of sanity and self-preservation, we might have to let some friendships change during waiting seasons. While some friendships will become closer, others will need a little more breathing room. It might seem as if we are growing apart for a time, as our lives take different paths. We don't have to be rude or cut people off, but we might talk a little less frequently. They might not be our primary confidants in our struggle with waiting. If we are wise—not tossing friendships out the window or saying hurtful things, just dialing back their intensity a bit—we can still preserve the relationships and circle back to them when life settles.

Give the Grace You Need

If he can't get us to give in to envy, Satan will try to hurt our relationships with another pesky temptation: hypersensitivity.

Our relationships—with roommates, coworkers, family, friends, church family, significant others—all go through upheaval as we grapple with our times of waiting. People fumble around and give painful, awkward, and downright insulting advice. They are insensitive. They hurt our feelings:

On the day you get the credit card bill to end all credit card bills, your sister shows you endless pictures of the renovations to her dream house.

On the day you feel most hopeless about your health, a coworker regales you with tales from her latest triathlon.

On the day you get overlooked (again) for a promotion, a close friend shares her awesome new job all over social media.

On the day you start your period, some well-meaning church lady tries to comfort you: "God's timing is perfect, honey, so it must not be your time. At least you have a husband. Be grateful for that."

Before you hammer these people—people you love—in the head, let's remember: everyone in our lives is going to say the wrong thing at some point. It's tempting to lash out at those who accidentally offend us, as if our not having a baby, or money, or health, or whatever, is their fault. But let's give these poor people a break.

Let's keep in mind: No matter how compassionate our friends are, they cannot understand exactly how we feel or anticipate our reactions to every comment. They won't know what to say sometimes. But hey—*we* don't know what to say to *ourselves* sometimes!

Is there ever a "right thing to say" to someone who lives with chronic pain?

Is there ever a "right thing to say" to a girl who thought she was getting engaged but broke up instead?

Is there ever a "right thing to say" to a woman who has spent all her savings on three rounds of failed in vitro fertilization?

We can choose to preserve our relationships by giving grace. Grace by the bucketful, grace by the ton. We can choose not to be so sensitive that we drive our friends and family away, however clueless they may be. As the waiting goes on, we are going to need those people more than we know, so let's show them the kind of grace we need *them* to show *us* right now.

Bear in mind: You are probably not saying all the right things yourself. You have probably made a few cynical, self-pitying remarks that your friends have chosen to overlook. You have probably been Debbie Downer at a party or two. You have probably monopolized some coffee dates with your waiting woes. And we *all* have said idiotic things to friends who were going through struggles we didn't understand. As James 3:2 observes, "Anyone who is never at fault in what they say is perfect, able to keep their whole body in check."

When you're tempted to resent people who don't understand, keep this in mind: During our waiting times, our friends and family offer us grace *even though they don't understand*. They look past our crazy, and try to listen, to understand, to empathize. Let's offer them the same grace in return. Let's pay grace forward. We will cash in on the deposit before long.

Ruth and Naomi saw each other at their best and worst. They shared death, displacement, despair. Ruth stayed with Naomi even when she had wrapped herself in bitterness, an early death shroud. The Bible doesn't show us all their in-between moments—hurt feelings, misunderstandings, arguments—but as human and hurting as they were, they must have weathered some pain and difficulty in their relationship. Nevertheless, they stuck together, fought through, and helped each other find a second chance at happiness.

My prayer for your waiting season friendships is this: May you find friends wise enough to know when to speak and when to listen, when to confront and when to console, when to laugh-cry and when to just cry, when to commiserate and when to caffeinate. Above all, may they always come bearing chocolate. And when it's their turn, may you turn and do the same for them.

That, my friends, is friendship.

Waiting Room Reading

For Further Study
Ruth and Naomi's story is found in the short book of Ruth. You can read more about David and Jonathan's friendship in 1 Samuel 18–20; 23:15–18; 31.

Journal Prompt
How do you feel about your current friendships? Would it help you to be more open with friends about how your wait is going? Is it time to expand your support system? Do you have ideas for new people to whom you can open up your heart? How do you feel about that: Excited? Nervous? Intimidated?

Prayer Prompt
The Lord makes firm the steps
  of the one who delights in him;
though he may stumble, he will not fall,
  for the Lord upholds him with his hand. . . .

The salvation of the righteous comes from the Lord;
  he is their stronghold in time of trouble.
The Lord helps them and delivers them;
  he delivers them from the wicked and saves them,
  because they take refuge in him.
Psalm 37:23–24, 39–40

8
Finding Joy in the Journey

Mary's Story
Treasured Things

Based on Luke 2:22–52

*H*ave you seen our son? Twelve years old, blue robe, black hair, thin as a reed? His name is Jesus. No?"

At every stall, the merchants shrug, shake heads no. Offer free samples.

As Joseph and Mary round the corner to the stalls nearest the temple, Mary's hands begin to shake. Three days' worth of fear and exhaustion are weighing her down. *We are running out of places to look.*

Joseph puts one arm around her shoulders, inviting her to lean in and draw from his strength, but she pulls away, pushes forward. She will rest when they find their son. Voices rise and twist, filling the air: "Dried figs!" "Goat cheese!" "Two doves, two coins!"

She pauses, caught in memory.

Snug in Mary's arms, eight-day-old Jesus makes soft sounds in His sleep. Joseph buys two doves for the sacrifice, and their new three-member family crosses the temple courtyard on their way to the baby's dedication. Through a gap in the river of people, a gnarled old man emerges, limps up to Mary. His eyes, faded but glistening, light on the bundle in her arms. He raises his voice. "Sovereign Lord, You may now dismiss Your servant Simeon in peace." Tears shine silver on his wrinkled cheeks as he prophesies: "This child is destined to cause the rising and falling of many in Israel." As the curious crowd presses in, staring, Simeon turns sad, milky eyes on Mary and speaks quiet words just for her: "Courage, my dear. A sword will pierce your own soul, too."

Shaking free of the memory, she starts in on the next merchant: "Have you seen—"

"Joseph! Mary!" The shout pierces the market hubbub. Joseph and Mary freeze, lock gazes.

Joseph says, "Is that—?"

"Yes," Mary breathes. "My brother's voice!"

Joseph calls out, "Here! We're here!"

"Joseph! This way!"

Mary chokes out a sound, half gurgle, half cry. Abandoning decorum, she grabs her skirts in her fists and sprints ahead of her husband. She emerges from the labyrinth of stalls, bursting out into the open area in the temple courtyard, and scans the crowd.

There! Beside one of the *mikveh*, the pools for ceremonial cleansing, she spots her brother's tall frame and multicolored robe, and beside him, a gangly boy in blue, all elbows and knees.

"Jesus!"

He spots her: "Mother!" Jesus runs forward, arms reaching—*on chubby baby legs one-year-old Jesus stumbles forward, arms reaching; one more step and He collapses into her arms, belly-laughing and beaming*— and they collide hard. On tiptoe she throws arms around His bony shoulders and squeezes with all her strength, as if she could fold Him back inside her womb for safekeeping. She is crying, laughing, shaking. "I thought—We couldn't—I don't—"

He twists in her arms, coughs into her neck. "Mother, please— can't—breathe."

Joseph's hand, warm on her shoulder, gives her a gentle tug back. She loosens her grip but keeps one hand clamped around her son's wrist, just in case. Her eyes conduct a frantic sweep, scrutinizing every inch from wavy hair to sandaled toe. When she sees He still has all the body parts he was born with, all apparently unharmed—*ten newborn fingers, ten newborn toes, she can't stop counting, can't stop tracing the lines of His scrunchy nose and rosebud lips; can't stop losing herself in His bright and blinking gaze, brand-new and innocent, ancient and wise*—

her breathing slows a little. Relief hits, a dizzying wave.

For the space of three blinks she smiles at Him, drinks Him in. But relief is swiftly swallowed by rage. She measures out words. "Where? Have? You? Been?" She skewers Him with a stare, as if she could drag the truth out through His eyeballs, though she has never known Him to lie.

His big brown eyes hold hers—as always, His are open windows to His feelings. Today they confess confusion, apology, regret.

"Why were you worried?" His baffled gaze skips from Mary to Joseph and back to Mary. "Didn't you know I had to be in my Father's house?" He waves long fingers toward the temple behind Him. Spares one longing glance over His shoulder.

"You *what*?" Mary gapes at Joseph, finding an echo of her own bewilderment on his face, though she thinks his mouth may be twitching with amusement behind his graying beard. She clears her throat and glares daggers at her husband. Taps her toe on the ground, fast. Insistent. Impatient.

Joseph takes the hint. "Son, I can't believe you treated us this way. What could you possibly have been doing in the temple for three days?"

The boy's eyes spark, and words spill out. "Oh! Rabbi Samuel was teaching his disciples about messianic themes through the Prophets, and I asked if I could sit in, and then we started tracing them through Isaiah, and. . ."

On and on He talks, faster and faster, until finally Joseph is chuckling and Mary is biting back an exasperated smile.

"Okay, okay, we believe you," Joseph says, reaching up a hand as if to muss his son's hair. Jesus ducks away, grinning.

Mary catches Jesus' cloak and pulls Him in, forcing another hug. "Hey!" He protests, laughing, but then He leans into her, bending down to rest His head on her shoulder. . .

She snatches Him up and nuzzles her nose into His tangled toddler curls—always they smell clean like soap and sweet like figs—and whispers, "I love you so much." Somber as a grown-up, like one making a vow, He lisps, "I love you so much, too." Flings pudgy arms around her neck. Melts into her, curving His small body into hers.

She speaks into his hair. "We're happy you love God's Word, son. Just tell us where you're going next time, okay?"

"I will. I'm so sorry I worried you."

"You'd better be." She elbows Him. "What do I do with you?"

He flashes His biggest, most charming grin and spreads His arms wide, as if to hug the world. "You'll just have to love me!"

The whole journey home, Mary relives His words about the temple, the Torah. The light in His eyes, the thrill on His face. She tucks His look, His words, His joy, the very *feel* of Him, into the sacred room in her heart reserved just for Him, her oldest child. The room that holds all her favorite *Jesus* memories.

But the closer they get to home, the louder Simeon's long-ago words echo in her mind, haunting her, taunting her: *Destined to cause the rising and falling of many.* For the thousandth time she wonders what those words might mean.

A sword will pierce your own soul, too. For the thousandth time, she tries *not* to wonder what those words might mean. Today she thinks she caught a glimpse.

She wonders how long she will have to wait to find out.

Poor Mary! I once lost a child in a park for two minutes, the longest, most agonizing 120 seconds I have ever lived. I can't imagine losing a child for three days. But Mary was in for much more hardship than this. As Simeon prophesied, a sword did pierce her own soul as Jesus grew and His purposes became clear.

If young Mary ever sat around dreaming about her future, we can be sure her five-year life plan did not include a visit from an angel, disgrace and near-divorce, birthing a miracle baby in a barn, fleeing her home in the middle of the night to save her baby's life. . . Her life didn't just face one unexpected curve in the road; she rode the Tail of the Dragon. (What's the Tail of the Dragon? It's an eleven-mile stretch of road in Deal's Gap, North Carolina: eleven miles, 318 curves, a biker's dream. Why do I know this? I'm the daughter of a Harley-riding preacher.) Mary had to choose how to think, how to adapt to a life plan she never would have planned for herself.

Although a cloud of uncertainty cast her future in shadow—what was God's will for her son's life, and hers, and what did Simeon's warning mean?—still she treasured small moments in the sun. Some were mysterious, miraculous, not yet fully understood, but she recognized their beauty and vowed to remember, to savor. What a great example, and practice, for all of us who live with uncertainty!

Waiting for Mr. Letterman Jacket

It's the summer after my sophomore year of college. I'm in summer school. What's the only good thing about summer school, about taking literature classes in hyperdrive, spending hours studying instead of sunbathing, reading twelve ancient novels in five weeks? It means I get to spend the summer months hanging out occasionally with Mr. Letterman Jacket, who has also stayed in town to practice with the football team.

One day he does something shocking: he initiates.

(I know this isn't a dating book, but want a random piece of potentially life-changing dating advice? If a boy is not initiating—if you only hang out when it's your idea, I'm sorry to tell you he isn't in love [yet]. When he starts initiating, the tide just might be turning in your favor.)

So he calls and invites me to a movie.

Alone.

We don't do alone. We are always in groups, circling each other like planets trying to find orbit, reading vibes across rooms.

Alone has to mean something, right?

He buys tickets and popcorn. This is feeling more and more like a date in disguise.

When the movie ends, the Dodge Avenger drives me back to my dorm. Just before we say good-bye—I'm already out of the car, leaning down to grab my purse—he leans across the passenger seat, looks up at me with those big caramel eyes, and says, "Hey."

My Spidey Senses start tingling. Is something about to happen?

Is he going to tell me how he feels? Does he finally actually *feel something*? Is my wait finally over? Or does he just want me to tutor him in English next year? (All this in 0.6 seconds.)

"Hey, I've been thinking about it, and—you really have become my best friend." He smiles, a big self-satisfied smile that seems to say, *You're welcome.*

My eyes narrow.

Best friend?

Best friend?

What is this, second grade?

What in the world am I supposed to do with that?

I don't want to be your best friend, bozo; that's what your offensive line is for.

So I smile and blink for a long time, trying—failing—to form a response. My best friend Sara's face pops into my mind—sorry, Mr. Letterman Jacket, I may be smitten, but you haven't bested my bestie yet, and I'm not going to pretend. I'm nothing if not honest, so I say, "You're—uh—one of my most special friends, too."

He makes a weird face.

I make a weird face.

We bid an extremely awkward good-bye.

And it's clear: I'm still waiting.

Mr. Letterman Jacket does not feel what I feel.

I am not going to have joy of the dating kind this summer; I'm going to have to adjust my expectations. Fill my time, my heart, with other people, other things. Find joy elsewhere.

Waiting for Perfect

I used to think I was the only one waiting for stuff, but gradually I came to realize that everybody is waiting for something. Even wealthy people and celebrities who don't seem to "need" anything. Even older people who appear to have life all figured out, all of their big life questions answered. Even that girl on Facebook with the great guy, 2.5 beautiful kids, 4,000 friends, granite countertops, and photos of her perfect family hitting life's milestones and highlights right on time.

Here's the truth: Nobody's life is perfect. Nobody has everything they want.

Life may never be perfect (what is "perfect" anyway?), and it certainly won't go according to our five-year plan. But it can still be full. Meaningful. Godly. Rich. Even fun.

Here's another truth, one I have fought hard to embrace: we don't have to wait for perfect to find joy. The opposite holds true, too: if we wait for perfect, we will never find joy.

Sometimes we can't imagine feeling happy unless life comes in the exact packaging we have chosen for ourselves. *I'll never be happy until. . . I can't be content unless. . .* We have to get rid of the rules we set for our joy, the *untils* and *unlesses*. This opens our hearts up to enjoy gifts, even happiness, from God—even if they come in a different form than we had imagined.

Little Ella has a journal, her Dear God Journal. Every night she writes a prayer. Most nights she writes, "Dear God, please give me a happy family. Everyone living in one house. No one sad or fighting. Amen." It's a prayer that can't be answered, can't ever be *yes*, because her family is already broken. Ella grows up. Learns to cherish, to enjoy, the family she has—stepparents, half siblings, occasional drama and all. She hangs her childhood hopes on building a marriage and family of her own, starting with a clean slate. But then she falls in love with a kind, godly man who has already suffered the agony of divorce, who already has two young children. As Ella falls deeper in love, past the point of no return, she realizes: *This will still be messy. It's not the picture-perfect, painful-history-free arrangement I thought I was waiting for, but it will be my story. Our story. And it can still be beautiful.* As Ella's friend and admirer, I say her family *is* beautiful. Messy sometimes but beautiful always.

Karen's two-year-old son, Daniel, is beautiful but silent. Big blue eyes, elfin cheekbones, delicate hands. She shuttles him from doctor to doctor, desperate for answers. Daniel's paperwork accrues a staggering number of medical terms and strange acronyms: comorbid issues, underdeveloped myelination, PDD-NOS. One day at an appointment, a secretary glances down at Daniel's paperwork and says—flippantly, like making small talk about the weather—"Ah, so your son has autism, and—"

Time stops.

Karen's heart stops.

Hope comes crashing down.

"My son has *what*? What did you say?"

The startled secretary blinks up at her, stammering, "I–I'm sorry. You don't know your son has autism? That's what PDD-NOS means."

Karen staggers home, heart splintering, future shattering.

For months she has convinced herself she was waiting (praying and pleading, seeking and shuttling, anguishing and advocating) to find her son healing, a permanent solution. Now she embarks on a different emotional journey, spending months—really years—praying for peace, fighting through denial and anger and fear and sorrow, learning to accept a different answer, embrace a different path: Daniel will make some improvements with time and treatment, but his conditions will never go away, not all the way, not the way she had hoped. This—speech delay, PDD-NOS, autism—this is his life. *Her* life, with her boy. Her beautiful boy—still beautiful, still hers, still deeply loved and daily enjoyed—acronyms, autism, and all. Today ten-year-old Daniel, with his quiet smiles and lightning-fast hugs, is the spark that lights Karen's world, the joy of her life. She calls him her gift.

No matter what you're waiting for, even if there is a hole in your heart where The Thing is meant to be, joy is still possible. Within reach. Even right here, right now—wherever *here* and *now* are for you, whatever they look like. Even without *it*—The Thing you are waiting for. Even if *it* turns out looking different than you had imagined.

Jesus promised, "I have come that they may have life, and have it to the full" (John 10:10). A full life in Christ doesn't always include a picket fence, a handsome prince, or a perfect bill of health—at least, not all at the same time! Time and again, Jesus reminds us to look ahead for our happiness, ahead to heaven and the next life. To find our treasures not in earthly things but in things that will last in the life to come. Things that will not spoil or fade. In His few, difficult years on this earth, He showed us how to find joy even in the midst of suffering and trial, imperfection and delay.

The Secrets No One Tells You about Happiness

Mary's example helps us grasp an important truth: *We can still choose joy, even while we are waiting,* even when our life feels like one ginormous question mark. It won't be easy, and we may endure many painful, tear-soaked days before journey's end, but even so, we don't have to live in a constant state of suspended joy. We can experience happiness all throughout our waiting seasons.

And here's a second secret for you, this one a brain bender: *We can be happy and sad at the same time.* Choosing joy doesn't mean the sad things in our lives have gone away. Choosing joy doesn't mean the grief, the loneliness, the depression, the sense of loss have disappeared altogether. As Proverbs 14:13 puts it, "Even in laughter the heart may ache." Life is rarely *all good* or *all bad.* Always, it's both. Two days before my first miracle baby was born, my dad announced he had prostate cancer. I have never experienced such profound sorrow, overwhelming fear, and exquisite joy all jammed into forty-eight hours.

Choosing joy means we decide to find, appreciate, celebrate, and keep focus on the joyful things in our lives. The more we focus on those things, the more they ease some of our sadness, blunting grief's sharp edges, making it bearable. The sadness still hovers, but it fades further into the background, allowing positive feelings to sharpen and take primary focus. Loss becomes a dull and manageable ache instead of a crippling, all-consuming, somebody-bring-me-morphine-now crisis.

Time out. Let's be clear on something: It's not sinful to feel sad or lonely. It's not wrong to grieve. No one wants you to ignore or brush aside your real feelings. They are valid, and many of them are unavoidable. But please, if you cannot manage feelings of depression, or if you are struggling with suicidal thoughts, *get professional help right away.* It's not unspiritual, faithless, or humanistic to seek help through medicine or therapy. Medicine and counseling, coupled with scripture and prayer, can be a powerful combination that helps us overcome emotional struggle. This chapter is about finding a way out. Not giving in. Fighting for joy in spite of pain. Redeeming waiting times. Stealing back joy when the odds are stacked against us. Okay? Okay. Time in.

So how can we choose joy even when our hearts ache? How can we hold on to some measure of happiness even during times of difficulty?

Joy Killers

We start reclaiming joy by resisting joy killers: feelings, thoughts, and temptations that automatically bring us down. That means taming our thoughts, taking them captive and making them obedient to Christ (2 Corinthians 10:5).

Even when life is good, going the way we want, happiness rarely *just happens*. Even in peaceful times, happiness is a choice. Our feelings are often the product of what we are thinking about, the perspective we choose to have. (Okay, they are also the product of our hormones, but that's another book altogether!)

So what are some of the joy killers we fight when we are waiting?

- Envy
- Bitterness
- Guilt
- Resentment—toward God or people
- Blaming ourselves for our circumstances
- Torturing ourselves with what-ifs
- Believing Satan's lies about waiting (lies like *God doesn't love you* or *God is angry with you*—for more on these, see chapter 4)
- Stubbornness
- Having tunnel vision: choosing to focus on only one area of our lives as a source of joy
- Giving into *untils* and *unlesses*, setting rules for our own happiness, rules like: "I'll never be happy until. . ." and "I can't be happy unless. . ."

As someone who wrestles daily (sometimes hourly) with wayward, not-always-Christlike thoughts, I have found that the best defense is a good offense. As Romans 12:21 puts it, "Do not be overcome by evil, but overcome evil with good."

We can sit around trying to resist the negative: *Don't be jealous of your friend's new job; Don't think that God is angry with you; Don't blame God for your disappointment. . .* Or we can flood our minds with positive thoughts.

Philippians 4:8 gives us an extensive list of the kinds of things God wants us to fill our minds with:

> *Finally, brothers and sisters, whatever is true, whatever is noble, whatever is right, whatever is pure, whatever is lovely, whatever is admirable—if anything is excellent or praiseworthy—think about such things.*

When I am battling negative thoughts, I make myself sit and list things that fit these descriptions, for example:

True: *God is good, His love never fails, I stand in Christ*

Lovely: *matching freckles on sibling noses, little girls twirling, Julie's handwriting on a card in my mailbox*

You get the idea. The simple act of listing positive things instantly changes our view of the world, our view of our lives.

Do Not Despise the Small Things

From there we can take this one step further: turn simple "positive thinking" into God-focused gratitude. Gratitude changes everything about how we wait and how we feel. Isn't that empowering? When we are waiting, we can feel completely out of control—like our lives are spinning away in a direction we despise. But let us draw comfort from the knowledge that although we can't control *how long* we wait, we can control *how* we wait. Maybe we can't name the date we get better, get the raise, or get the break, but we can name the date we reclaim joy, and *it can be today.*

Not sure how to start? Here's a simple exercise that helps me: Make joy and gratitude a deliberate part of your day. Start and end your day with a few minutes of directed thinking. I find this practice especially helpful when I catch myself overgeneralizing. What's over-generalizing? A few bad things happen in one day; therefore, *everything that day was bad.* Overgeneralizing allows one or two small negative moments too much power and influence, casting a pall over all the good. Directed thinking forces me to have a more balanced perspective and remember all the good in each day.

Try this. In the morning, write down:

- three things you have to look forward to today or
- three things you are thankful for this morning.

(Some days you might be pushing it. Your thankful list might be "The sun still hangs in the sky," or "I woke up in a bed this morning," or even "I woke up. Period." But hey—we take what we can get.)

Before you go to bed, write down:

- three positive things that happened today or
- three ways you saw God at work today.[1]

Remember, even simple things like "The ice cream lady gave me an extra scoop of ice cream" count. Small blessings are still blessings. As Zechariah 4:10 says, "Who dares despise the day of small things?"

Unexpected Ice Cream

Jeremiah 17, the famous passage about depending on God, includes an intriguing turn of phrase. It reads:

> *The man who trusts in mankind,*
> *who makes human flesh his strength*
> *and turns his heart from the* Lord *is cursed.*
> *He will be like a juniper in the Arabah;*
> he cannot see when good comes
> *but dwells in the parched places in the wilderness.*
>
> Verses 5–6 hcsb, emphasis added

The emphasized phrase reveals a powerful insight: When we are focused on ourselves and not depending on God, we *cannot see the good things God gives us.* We cannot see our blessings even when God drops them directly in our laps! Sometimes we are prospering *even while we wait,* but we are too focused on ourselves and our problems—too exhausted from the journey, too obsessed with what we *don't* have—to even notice what we *do* have, the other blessings God has already given.

Because all of our relatives live in different cities, our family takes a lot of loooooong road trips. As long as I have had my Starbucks mocha for the day, I'm kind of a "Let's suck it up and keep moving and munching on almonds" kind of road tripper, but my husband is a sucker for McDonald's ice cream sundaes (which are not really ice cream, if you ask me, but I digress). Every few hours, he likes to stop at random McDonald's restaurants and give our kids sugar highs by buying them fake ice cream. They are delighted (and extremely hyper) every time, because the next best thing to being there—wherever we are going—and being done with the waiting, done with the journey, is unexpected ice cream! Free, unplanned sugar! Sometimes when we are waiting, I think God is like Kevin: He randomly lets us pause our journey, and He buys us bonus ice cream. Just because it makes the trip less painful. Just because He loves us and likes to see us smile.

In chapter 10 we will take a look at Joseph's journey to see how God prospered him even during times of extreme loss and hardship. Genesis 39:3 tells us that even in slavery "the LORD was with him and. . .gave him success in everything he did." Joseph's life shows us how God often deals with us, His people: He doesn't always change our circumstances for us, but He gives us blessings that make painful situations bearable.

Deuteronomy 2:7 provides another example of God's faithfulness and kindness even through prolonged hardship:

> *The LORD your God has blessed you in all the work of your hands. He has watched over your journey through this vast wilderness. These forty years the LORD your God has been with you, and you have not lacked anything.*

A few chapters later we read:

> *Your clothes did not wear out and your feet did not*
> *swell during these forty years. Know then in your heart*
> *that as a man disciplines his son, so the LORD your God*
> *disciplines you.*

DEUTERONOMY 8:4–5

Spending forty years wandering around the desert, burying their parents and grandparents, wasn't a happy experience for the Israelites, and yet here God assures them that He was with them—even blessing them—as they waited and wandered. He watched over their journey, met their needs, sustained them. He even paid attention to details, keeping them healthy and clothed.

What about your life this waiting season? Maybe God hasn't yet given you The Thing, but while you wait, is He giving you *other* things to encourage you, boost your spirits, and ease the pain of the journey? Has He bought you any unexpected ice cream?

God's Kind of Joy

I reread the Beatitudes again this week, in light of waiting, and I was struck anew: God doesn't value what the world values. The world values tangible blessings because those are all they have. Christians have so much more to look forward to. We can—and do—experience great blessings in this world, but we hold on to them lightly. We recognize the fragility and temporary nature of this life. Our true hope and greatest joys lie in the next world. Every joy here is but a shadow of the joys to come, a foretaste of eternity with God.

Jobs end.

Money spends.

People move away or pass away.

Heaven is forever.

The Weirdest Kind of Joy

Let's take another look at the familiar James 1 passage:

Consider it a great joy, my brothers, whenever you experience various trials, knowing that the testing of your faith produces endurance. But endurance must do its complete work, so that you may be mature and complete, lacking nothing. . . .

A man who endures trials is blessed, because when he passes the test he will receive the crown of life that God has promised to those who love Him.

VERSES 2–4, 12 HCSB

This scripture makes me squirm. Consider it a great joy whenever I experience trials? Really? When I think *great joy*, I don't think *suffering*, and I definitely don't think *waiting*. (Let's also keep in mind that many early Christians who read this letter before us endured persecution to a degree many modern Christians can't even fathom.) When I think about times of great joy, I think *getting what I want*. I think *life going my way*. I think *perfect everything*. That's when I feel joyful. So yeah, this passage is a tough one.

But James insists that suffering of all kinds (and certainly, waiting is a type of suffering) makes us better. It makes us grow. And growth brings joy. . .or at least it can if we let it.

When I think about how good it feels to know I am growing—becoming stronger, humbler, more faithful, more patient, more compassionate, less worldly—then I see what God means here. I get it.

Fighting the What-Ifs

I admit: I'm a catastrophizer. You might even say I have Worst-Case Scenario Disorder. My happy train derails the minute I lend power to two dangerous words: *what if*.

It goes like this: One of my kids spikes a sudden high fever. I start thinking, *What if. . . ?* In seconds I have played out a horrific mental drama: The child goes into febrile seizures, we rush to the hospital but it's too late, they fall into a coma, which they survive, but barely—they have irreversible brain damage, they spend the rest of their days in a semivegetative state, I go to work overtime to pay their medical bills, but I don't earn enough, so we end up in a homeless shelter, the strain makes me neglect my other kids and my marriage. . . I die alone on the streets.

Yep. I can get from a kid's fever to bankruptcy, homelessness, and death on the streets in twenty-six seconds. (You think I'm kidding or exaggerating? I am completely serious!) I try to tell myself that a vivid imagination is a great quality for a writer to have, but sometimes (*sigh*) I wish mine was less forceful. Or at least less pessimistic—it never runs free in a positive direction: we win the lottery, which allows us to fund a cure for cancer, and the whole world holds hands and sings "Kumbaya."

When we are waiting, if we want to hang on to joy, we can't give in to catastrophizing. We can't live in the land of *what if*, always worrying about what comes next, what could happen. To put this in scriptural terms, Jesus gently reminds us, "Do not worry about tomorrow, for tomorrow will worry about itself. Each day has enough trouble of its own" (Matthew 6:34).

Let's not give in to the temptation to play out long-term catastrophic scenarios: *What if I never get The Thing? What if life never changes?*

Let's take life the way God meant us to take it—one day at a time—treasuring small joys, thanking Him for providing the manna we need to make it through today.

The Power of "Yet"

And perhaps we can tweak our inner mental terminology to allow more room for positive outcomes. Instead of thinking *I have not found Mr. Right; therefore it is safe to assume I will never find him, and I will die alone with my microwave dinners and cat collection*, why not think *I have not found Mr. Right* yet? Why not think. . .

I haven't overcome anxiety yet.
I haven't gotten out of debt yet.
My child hasn't turned to God yet.

Yet is a powerful word. It makes room for hope and room for God. Three small letters, so much possibility.

I know. *Yet* scares me, too. Hope scares me, too. *Yet* makes me get my hopes up more than I want to. We recognize, in making *yet* statements, that we can't predict God's plans for our future, and we don't *know* if we will receive what we are waiting for, but allowing the *possibility* helps us fight despair. It keeps us from mourning prematurely, or worse, giving up before God has actually said no. We allow room for God to work.

I love the attitude Shadrach, Meshach, and Abednego expressed before they were thrown into the fiery furnace:

> *"If we are thrown into the blazing furnace, the God we serve is able to deliver us from it, and he will deliver us from Your Majesty's hand. But* even if he does not, *we want you to know, Your Majesty, that we will not serve your gods or worship the image of gold you have set up."*
> Daniel 3:17–18, emphasis added

They held on to hope that God could still save them, still answer their prayers—they hadn't been rescued *yet*—but recognizing that rescue wasn't a given, they surrendered to God's decision. They held on to hope and surrender, two conflicting emotions, at the same time.

Living Mountaintop to Mountaintop

We tend to live highlight to highlight. We mark our lives by epic moments: first boyfriend, graduation, first job, engagement, wedding day, big promotion, first kid. . . But most of life is lived in the in-between.

We make a big deal about college graduation, but it's *college itself* that's the worthwhile experience. Those four years (*cough*—or five, or six, or—okay, we'll stop there) are what matters: the things you learn, the people you meet, the memories you make, the ways you mature.

We long for a Pinterest-perfect wedding day, but a marriage is so much more than a wedding day. All the months or years spent dating—the date nights, the stupid jokes, the sweet nothings—it all adds up to a *relationship*. The greatest joy is in the marriage itself, not in the wedding day.

Mountaintop experiences—getting a promotion, getting engaged, buying a house, having a baby, moving to your dream city—don't come along that often in life. When they come, they are glorious, and we should stand on that mountaintop and praise the goodness of God at the top of our lungs. Like David, let's sing our hearts out when God comes through and prayers are answered. Let's take a million pictures with our hearts and minds—maybe even take a few with our phones. But let's remember that most of life is lived between mountaintops, struggling from one peak to the next, with many dark valleys and rocky detours between. Life *is* the journey. And even as we hike, if we will stop and look around and live in the moment, we will be treated to breathtaking views.

To laughter with friends.

To obstacles overcome.

To talks around campfires.

To storms proclaiming the power of God.

To struggles that become stories we tell for the rest of our lives.

Let's find joy in our journeys, wherever they may lead, however winding, however many detours, however long the space between mountaintops.

As you continue your journey through your waiting wilderness, try these simple decisions on for size:

- I choose to hold on to hope for the life I want, while choosing to find joy in the life I already have.
- I choose to keep praying for the blessings I want and need but to remain grateful for the blessings I already have.
- Like Mary, I choose to put life on pause. To notice the small treasures each day holds. To tuck them away in a secret place in my heart and draw them out again and again to remember the goodness of God, to relive His kindness, and to rejoice in the richness that's already mine.

Waiting Room Reading

For Further Study
More of Mary's story can be found in Matthew 1–2, Luke 1–2, Mark 3:20–35, and Acts 1:14.

Journal Prompt
How do you see God taking care of you while you are waiting? Have you received any unforeseen blessings along the way? Have you received love or care from an unexpected source? What are some positive memories you will take away from this waiting season?

Prayer Prompt
I remain confident of this:
*   I will see the goodness of the LORD*
*   in the land of the living.*
Wait for the LORD;
*   be strong and take heart*
*   and wait for the LORD.*
PSALM 27:13–14

9
When Faith Starts Fading

Gideon's Story
Mighty Warrior

Based on Judges 6

𝒯he sun is a molten coin, heat dripping down. Gideon's neck and shoulders sizzle and scald. He climbs out of the winepress where he has spent the day hiding and working, working and hiding. He drags a cover over the opening to make sure the Midianites don't discover the wheat he has been threshing. Wheat his family needs to survive.

A chuckle sounds behind him.

Gideon whirls around, hand on the dagger at his waist.

A tall man sits perched on the lowest branch of his father's favorite oak, partially hidden in dappled shade. Unfolding long limbs, the man drops to the ground and steps into full sun, a smile spreading wide across his face. He holds both palms up to show he is unarmed. "The Lord is with you, mighty warrior!"

Gideon looks behind, over his shoulder—no one there—then levels a skeptical look on the stranger. "Sorry, did you mean—you don't mean *me*?"

The man nods.

Gideon smiles easy; he is used to being teased. He can play along. He shrugs, flashes a self-deprecating grin. "Ah yes, mighty warrior, that's me. Gideon the Wheat Warrior, at your service." He bows grandly. "There's not a head of grain I can't separate from its stalk." He mimes brandishing a scythe.

The stranger smiles, keeping his eyes locked on Gideon. Gideon grows restless under the weight of his gaze, swipes sweat from his forehead. "You gotta quit looking at me like that. So. . .I'm going inside to eat. You have a nice day. Enjoy my father's tree."

The stranger measures his words, gives each one a kick: "The Lord is with you, mighty warrior."

Gideon crosses his arms with a sigh and resists the urge to roll his eyes. "Okay, fine. I'll bite. If the Lord is with us, then why all this?" He gestures at the covered winepress, his father's stripped fields. "Why has the Lord abandoned us? My grandfather told a thousand stories about God's great deeds when He rescued our people from Egypt, but now people say God has either run out of miracles or run out of town." He shrugs one shoulder. "Friend, I don't know where you've been the past seven years, but the Lord left us a long time ago." He taps a thumb on the hilt of his dagger and drops his voice, speaking half to himself. "But believe me—when He returns, I'll be at the front of the line welcoming Him back."

The man studies the fields then turns to look at Gideon, a gaze hotter than sun. "Go in the strength you have and save Israel out of Midian's hand. Am I not sending you?"

Gideon shakes his head. "If you're looking to recruit guys to pick a fight with Midian, you've come to the wrong house. Around here, we keep our heads down and stay out of trouble."

The man says nothing, only lifts an eyebrow.

Gideon shifts his weight. "I stopped playing warrior with wooden swords years ago. If you value your life, you'll do the same."

The man stares Gideon down until he looks away, feels the burn of shame rising in his cheeks. Defensive, not sure why he is taking this stranger seriously, he says, "How can *I* save Israel? You must be new, or else you'd know my clan is weakest in Manasseh and I'm least in my family. They stick me in there"—he points at the wine-press—"doing work no one else wants. Wheat Warrior, remember?" His laugh comes strained.

Something flashes in the man's eyes. "I will be with you, and you will strike down all the Midianites together. None will survive." A cold wind gusts, raising hairs on the back of Gideon's neck. In blue sky, thunder rolls.

Realization dawns, a sickening thrill. Gideon grasps at words, tries to steady his shaking hands. "My Lord—I didn't—didn't realize. . ." He licks his lips, looks around for help, as if his father might appear, tell him what to do. "If—If I've really found favor in your eyes, give me a sign that it is really you talking to me. Please don't leave"— he waves a hand at the house—"I'd like to bring an offering."

The man inclines his head and settles again under the tree.

Gideon rushes inside trembling, thoughts flying.

Has the Lord really come to save us?

Why does he keep calling me "warrior"?

Did he get the wrong house?

He pauses, heart sinking.

That's it.

Wrong house.

I'll feed him and point him down the road to Nathan's sons.

But as his hands work dough, making bread without yeast, his thoughts and his body disagree. His mind says, *No—this is a mistake—run while we can*; his body says, *Yes—we've been waiting for this—we fight to the death.*

His muscles hum with a dizzying energy he doesn't recognize. He tries to resist but it's sweeping him away, he is drinking it in, already gone.

His eyes keep straying to his father's sword where it hangs, gleaming, over the door.

Keeping watch.

Waiting.

Calling him.

Mighty warrior.

I adore Gideon. When I hear his questions to God's messenger, I feel as though I have found my faith twin: he longs to believe, tries to believe, but is plagued by insecurity and doubt.

In Gideon's defense, life hasn't given him many reasons for great faith. When a foreign nation descends on your homeland—stealing crops, stripping dignity—doubt burrows, a dangerous seed. When you spend seven years watching all the heroes you admire humiliated and hiding, some bowing to different gods, the seed sprouts, takes root.

You can hear doubt threaded all through Gideon's words to the angel: "If the Lord is with us. . ."

It's a big word, *if*.

"Why has the Lord abandoned us?"

It's an even bigger word, *abandoned*.

Gideon isn't sure God is with His people anymore. He doesn't even recognize the angel at first. Gideon doubts God, but he also doubts himself: "My clan is the weakest. . . I am the least. . ."

Ever felt that way—less than—because God hasn't yet given the blessing you seek? Everyone you know is enjoying God's blessings (they must be—look at the pictures on social media!) while you lag behind, the weakest, the least? *Maybe it's my fault. Maybe I don't deserve God's presence. Maybe I'm not worth a miracle.*

In Gideon's journey from winepress to mighty warrior (Judges 6–8), we find a beautiful story of God's grace and patience toward one who doubts. (And all the doubters like me say, "Amen"!)

Let's use Gideon's doubts as a springboard for addressing a few of our own.

1. "If the Lord is with us, why has all this happened to us?"

Gideon had his *if*; we have ours:

If the Lord is with me. . .

Why am I still sick?

Why am I still anxious?

Why did I lose my job?

When we are waiting, we might also flip this phrase around, like so:

If the Lord is with me. . .

Why *haven't* I gotten well?

Why *haven't* I found relief?

Why *haven't* I landed The Job?

The underlying problem here? We don't realize it, but we fall prey to misguided expectations, a sort of if-then theology:

If I am righteous, then God will bless me.

If I believe, then God will give me what I ask.

If I am a Christian, then my life will be happy.

More specifically. . .

If I don't flirt with worldly guys, then God will give me a godly boyfriend.

If I delight myself in God, then God will open my child's heart to Him.

If I pray with faith, then I will get well.

It's not that these if-then statements aren't true. It's just that they aren't *always* true. They aren't money-back guarantees. Waiting forces us to mature in our thinking. It makes us move past simplistic if-then theology.

Are such things blessings from God? Absolutely. Are they iron-clad promises from God? Well. . .not exactly, not every time. (Ever known a Christian to die of illness in spite of thousands of prayers by faithful people?)

The problem is, when we get our expectations confused, we feel let down by God. Disappointed. Hurt. Maybe even betrayed. Hurt and betrayal open us up to doubt and anger. Left unchecked, doubt and anger put our very walk with God at risk.

Let's take a deeper look at sources of doubt by examining two famous if-then statements in the Bible. These two passages have twisted my faith into knots during waiting seasons:

If-then statement number one:

Then the disciples came to Jesus in private and asked, "Why couldn't we drive it out?"

He replied, "Because you have so little faith. Truly I tell you, if you have faith as small as a mustard seed, you can say to this mountain, 'Move from here to there,' and it will move. Nothing will be impossible for you."

MATTHEW 17:19–21

Okay, so we all know this one, and it's problematic, especially when you're going through a season of waiting. "If you have faith. . .[then] you can say. . ."

First of all, how many of us tried as children to pray mountains into the oceans and were secretly heartbroken when the mountains stayed put? Yeah, I feel your eight-year-old pain.

But how many of us have also struggled with this idea that we are basically guaranteed to receive *anything* from God if we believe? And Jesus isn't asking here for perfect faith—only a mustard seed will do! So then why aren't we receiving more of the things we are asking for? Why are so many of us "mustard-seeding" but still waiting?

Here's where we get tangled up inside: We start by scrutinizing our own faith, blaming ourselves—*O me of little faith!* We beat up on ourselves for a while, trying to flog ourselves into greater faith. After a while, if nothing changes, we may begin to doubt Jesus' words, and here's where it gets dangerous. If we can't trust Jesus' words, then is the whole Christianity thing a sham?

Before we all flip out, let's reason this one out step-by-step. First, have you ever heard of a mountain being prayed into the ocean? I haven't. Surely, if Jesus was being literal here, the whole mountain-jumping business would have happened at least once in the two thousand years since Jesus made the promise, right? *Someone* would have mustered the mustard seed of faith required to make it happen? Hmm. Apparently not.

Analogies, Hyperbole

Let's keep in mind that we have to be careful in how we interpret illustrations and analogies. Illustrations and analogies are meant to teach us by painting word pictures or drawing comparisons, but they are by nature imperfect approximations of truth. And remember, Jesus is employing hyperbole here (*hyperbole* is just a fancy word for exaggeration). Yep. Jesus is exaggerating. When we say Jesus is exaggerating, we don't mean He is being dishonest; we mean He is being *dramatic*. Painting a memorable picture. Maybe even trying to get His disciples to laugh at a surprising image in the middle of a discouraging situation. (They were having this private conversation because the disciples had just publicly tried, and publicly failed, to drive out a demon that was endangering a young boy's life—talk about a moment in desperate need of a little levity.)

Okay, so even if Jesus isn't encouraging us to pray literal mountains into literal seas, we still have a problem. Even if we are not trying to move mountains, Jesus promises us that our prayers can do anything! *Anything!* "Nothing is impossible!" Right? *Right?*

Yes. No. Maybe.

Again, we have to be careful not to force Jesus' words into a super-literal box. What's the overall point of His words here? The big-picture message? Jesus' main point is that there are no limits to the power of prayer when it is coupled with faith. To put it another way, prayer is powerful because *God* is powerful.

Our faith matters. Great faith, paired with God's power, can bring about awesome things. Anything God wants. On the other hand, a lack of faith can limit God's actions. Like it or not, our faith makes a difference.

However, it would be simplistic, maybe even dangerous, to suggest that every time a person makes a request and pairs it with a small amount of faith, God is obligated to say yes. That kind of wooden interpretation makes *us* God instead of God! It makes God prisoner to our prayers, like a genie in a bottle. If that interpretation were valid, then half the world would have won the lottery by now! Or consider this extreme: we could pray for things that are against the will of God (praying injury on our enemies, for example), and as long as we have faith, then God would have to violate His own nature, His own rules, in order to obey *our* command.

The relationship between our faith, our prayers, and God's will is complex and nuanced. Bottom line, we need to understand this: God is powerful enough to do anything—even hurl a mountain into the sea—but He always reserves the right to say no to our requests. He can do anything, but He is free not to do it. He is God; we are not.

If-then statement number two:

> Delight yourself in the LORD,
>   and he will give you the desires of your heart. . . .
>
> Be still before the LORD and wait patiently for him.
>   PSALM 37:4, 7 NIV 1984

The if-then is implied here: *If* you delight, *then* God will give. We mentioned this, the crown jewel of the waiting passages, in chapter 1, and it deserves further exploration. I still remember a spring break trip I took with friends, smack in the middle of my pining-after-Mr. Letterman-Jacket days. I went for a prayer walk on the beach, read Psalm 37, and had a moment of "epiphany": *I know why The Boy hasn't fallen in love with me yet: I'm not delighting in God enough! My morning devotion times have been weak lately—if I'll just get it together and read and pray harder, then everything will work out.*

I had an emotional prayer there on the beach, promised to cling more tightly to God, gently reminded Him that I was in love with a certain boy—and then, having "repented," I half expected Mr. Letterman Jacket to show up at my dorm with flowers and chocolate the moment I got home.

Perhaps I was reading a bit too much into this passage, eh?

Here's the thing about Psalms: It's a book of poetry and prayer. Poetry prayers. Prayer poems. You get the idea. Poetry is not meant to be read in the same way other literature is read. Poets employ figurative language like metaphor and simile: "Hide me in the shadow of your wings"—but does God actually have wings (Psalm 17:8)? "Your word is a lamp for my feet"—but is the Bible part flashlight (Psalm 119:105)? You get the idea.

Writers of poetry also employ hyperbole and make frequent use of generalizations. That is, they state general truths about God, His Word, and His ways. They make observations about God and His ways that hold true *most of the time.* They observe general principles of how God works. But poetry is not intended to be taken in the same way as, for example, the Ten Commandments.[1]

So when the psalmist celebrates God granting our desires when we delight in Him, he is noting that in general this holds true. If you think about it, I bet you'll agree that this principle has proven true in your life. When we delight in God, our life goes better overall. We get more of the things that make us happy. Not all of the things all of the time, but many of the things. Maybe even most of the things most of the time.

I have spent more than a decade working hard and begging God for specific things in my writing career. Along the way, I have amassed more rejections than I can number, because it's not healthy to keep counting rejections once you pass seventy. But do those *nos* mean I'm not delighting enough in God? That He is displeased with me in some way? I don't think so. I can always grow in my walk with God, but this isn't a direct if-then relationship: *If* I delight in God, *then* He will always say yes to my prayers. It's just more complicated than that.

Managing Expectations

This leads us to a hugely important topic: expectations. Specifically, what we expect out of God and Christianity.

Somewhere along the way, we have bought into this idea that if we become a Christian, then all our dreams will come true. If we "give up" our lives for God, in return He will give us *everything we want*. Of course we wouldn't phrase it like that, but secretly—maybe even unconsciously—it's what we think. What we expect. In the quiet places of our hearts, we think Christians are supposed to have a good life, a happy life. We are God's people, His children! We know we don't deserve salvation, but even so we think we should get pretty much all of the things we pray for. We are not asking to be billionaires or anything, but we assume God will give us the basics: long life, college degree, happy marriage, healthy kids, solid career, decent house in a good school district. Right?

That's why we are shocked when God says wait. That's why we are devastated, maybe even angry, when He says no. That's why waiting and suffering can lead to serious doubt.

So what can we expect out of our faith? Take a look at this mind-blowing description of our rich life in Christ:

How blessed is God! And what a blessing he is! . . .
(What pleasure he took in planning this!) He wanted
us to enter into the celebration of his lavish gift-giving
by the hand of his beloved Son.

Because of the sacrifice of the Messiah, his blood
poured out on the altar of the Cross, we're a free
people—free of penalties and punishments chalked up
by all our misdeeds. And not just barely free, either.
Abundantly free! He thought of everything, provided
for everything we could possibly need, letting us in on
the plans he took such delight in making.

EPHESIANS 1:3, 6–9 MSG

God has already given us His best, and His best is all we need. He has given us His Son: "For God so loved the world that he gave his one and only Son" (John 3:16). He has given us Himself: "I am your shield, your very great reward," He told Abraham (Genesis 15:1). *God Himself* is our reward, and once we become Christians, we have Him, already and always. He is our Father, our Savior, our Friend.

More (amazingly, there's more!), we have salvation, the Spirit, "every spiritual blessing" (Ephesians 1:3), "everything we need to live and to serve God" (2 Peter 1:3 EXB). Anything else, any blessing this side of heaven, is just gravy. (That's what we say here in the South—oh, how we love our gravy!) The jobs, the family, the money, the comfortable lives we seek—while those are not necessarily sinful requests to make, they are bonuses. Let us learn the crucial difference in hoping for something given versus expecting something owed. The difference between a gift and a paycheck.

Certainly, Christianity offers us gifts past counting, joy beyond measure. . .but the blessings we prize are different from the world's. Our greatest blessings are often intangible. They are internal blessings affecting our hearts and our relationships, more than outward gifts like wealth and success.

Perhaps we should reconsider how we define being "blessed by

God." Maybe if we learn to look with different eyes, we will realize how blessed we *already are*. Because you don't yet have a husband, does that mean you are not richly blessed by your heavenly Father? Because I haven't yet gotten some career breaks I wanted, does that mean God is holding out on me? Because my father-in-law has been fighting cancer off and on for nearly twenty years, does that mean he is not living in God's favor? I say no. God says no. Even as we wait for God to answer some of our requests—even the deep-rooted desires that affect our identity and daily happiness—I pray we learn to recognize, and gratefully enjoy, the blessings He has already bestowed.

2. "Where are all his wonders that our ancestors told us about?"
You can hear conflict roiling in Gideon's heart as he challenges the angel, seeking proof. Evidence. Miracles. He has heard the stories, but his own experience has been different. Discouraging. Confusing.

Ever been there? Striving for faith, clawing for hope, but when you look for indications of God's faithfulness and power in your own history, the evidence stacks thin?

As time goes on, doubt's roots dig deeper:

Maybe God has changed.

Maybe Jesus can't be trusted.

Let's take a closer look at another problematic passage, a statement Jesus made to His disciples the night before He died:

> *"Very truly I tell you, whoever believes in me will do the works I have been doing, and they will do even greater things than these, because I am going to the Father.*
> *And I will do whatever you ask in my name, so that the Father may be glorified in the Son. You may ask me for anything in my name, and I will do it."*
>
> JOHN 14:12–14

Ever stumbled over this one? I have, especially during my waiting seasons: "Aha! See? Jesus is promising to do whatever I ask in His name. So, why don't I have what I want?" Before we all start banging our foreheads against our Bibles in frustration, let's break this down.

Keep the audience in mind.

We first have to consider the context: This was a promise Jesus made at a private dinner with the Twelve on the night of His arrest. He was preparing these men, close friends and daily companions, to carry on His mission in His absence. He was comforting them and equipping them with spiritual tools they would need to spread the Word and build His church.

Keep this crucial detail in mind: Jesus spoke these words in private to His disciples. It's not clear whether His words in this particular conversation also extend and apply to you and me in the same way. These men enjoyed a unique relationship with Jesus, and special privileges—power, understanding, and intimacy, among other things—accompanied their role. It is possible that these words were intended for these particular men and not for all Christians. (It's interesting to note that Jesus' words about how a mustard seed of faith can make a mountain go swimming were also spoken in private to His disciples.)

What's the point?

Take a look at a key phrase here: "so that the Father may be glorified in the Son." What is the purpose of Jesus' promise here? To make the Twelve happy? To make all their dreams come true? To give them true love, happy lives, healthy bodies, nice homes, worldly riches? No. The purpose of this promise is to glorify God.

While I don't think God has any problem with us asking Him for earthly blessings that will make us happy in this life, His greatest concern is with *His* glory, not our temporary pleasures.

But wait a second: Am I suggesting that prayers for a boyfriend or a baby or a job are worldly or sinful? Of course not. God Himself designed marriage, parenthood, and work—blessings all. A godly dating relationship or marriage can help God accomplish His will through us. From the moment He created humans, God recognized our need for companionship, and Solomon observed that two can be better than one (Ecclesiastes 4:9). (I say there's no harm in humbly mentioning these facts next time you pray to find The Guy!) Praying for a baby? Motherhood is a beautiful role, allowing us to fulfill our God-given nature and gifts as women. Praying for a job? A job helps us meet our own needs and meet others' needs; a career can fulfill us and allow us to develop and use our God-given skills for His glory. It's not wrong to ask for these things, and many times God is happy to give them to us.

As we make requests of God, let's keep in mind that His goals are bigger than our temporary comfort. He prioritizes holiness above happiness. It's not that God is opposed to joy or that happiness in itself is somehow wrong (I really, really like being happy!), it's just not God's primary goal.

3. "Give me a sign that it's really you."

> The LORD answered, "I will be with you, and you will strike down all the Midianites, leaving none alive."
> Gideon replied, "If now I have found favor in your eyes, give me a sign that it is really you talking to me."
> JUDGES 6:16–17

Deliverance comes to Gideon at last—the messenger of the Lord standing before him—but at first he can't see. He is so wounded, at first he can't believe.

Facing disappointment and delay for many months or many years can damage something inside. We build a protective wall to guard against heartache. We blunt the edges of our emotions, refusing to fully feel, in case we get hurt again. We read past God's promises—the ones where God declares His love for us, His grace, His kindness—because we just *can't* anymore. Like Gideon in the winepress, we are held hostage by fear and hesitation. We still doubt, still need encouragement.

In this chapter we have tackled doubt by considering a new perspective on if-then theology, by showing that some of the Bible's "promises" are not exactly promises, but rather gifts. Even so, I hope you will open your eyes to see and your heart to embrace the promises that *are* there, that *are* true. The promises you can always rely on, even in darkest of times:

Not worldly wealth, but spiritual, emotional, and relational riches.

Not a problem-free life, but strength and comfort and shelter to see you through problems when they come.

Not everything you want every time, but everything you need without fail.

I hope, like Gideon, you will look into the eyes of the Lord's messenger and realize God is trustworthy and safe, patient and kind.

Courage in the Dark

God shows up at Gideon's house. Calls him *warrior*. Rains heavenly fire.

You might think a personal invitation and commission from God would instantly fill your faith tank full, but that's not the case with Gideon. He is *more* faithful now but still afraid. Insecure. In need of reassurance.

> *That same night the Lord said to him, ". . . Tear down your father's altar to Baal and cut down the Asherah pole beside it. Then build a proper kind of altar to the Lord your God. . . ."*
>
> *So Gideon took ten of his servants and did as the Lord told him. But because he was afraid of his family and the townspeople, he did it at night rather than in the daytime.*
>
> Judges 6:25–27

Out of the winepress, into the fire. Gideon does what God commands, a daring act of defiance and leadership, but he does it at night, because he is afraid. He is still growing in faith, rising to fulfill the leadership position God wants him to take.

Several times in Gideon's story, doubt returns. He needs extra encouragement from God. And you know what's amazing? God gives it to him! God is patient, gently leading him, gradually building his faith. (See the story of the fleeces in Judges 6:36–40.)

Out of the winepress, into the war. The night before battle, as Gideon prepares to lead a force of only three hundred men against an army of many thousands, God anticipates Gideon's fear. This time Gideon doesn't even have to ask for proof of God's presence; God volunteers it: "If you are afraid to attack, go down to the camp with your servant Purah and listen to what they are saying. Afterward, you will be encouraged to attack" (Judges 7:10–11).

Gideon's story gives me hope for the many, many times my faith has faded, faltered, and failed. Gideon shows me that God can still use—still bless—doubters. Through Gideon I see the patience of our Father. The kindness. The high expectations. I see His willingness to work with, through, in spite of, and all around our weakness.

I see that our faith in God is important, but—heretical as it sounds—not *most* important. Most important is the faith *God has in us*—even when we are still doubting. Still afraid. Still hiding out, threshing wheat in winepresses.

Even when we cower in the winepress, God calls us mighty warriors.

He sees who we can be. Who we will be.

God is calling you, friend.

Out of doubt and fear and insecurity.

Out of the winepress, into the war.

Out of hiding, into His arms.

Waiting Room Reading

For Further Study
Gideon's story can be found in Judges 6–8. For another encouraging story about a doubter who found faith, read John 20:20–29. (Pay special attention to verse 29—it's talking about you and me!)

Journal Prompt
Is waiting exposing some holes in your faith that need filling? Is it

bringing up some questions about God? List your questions, along with ideas for scriptures and books that might help you address them. Do you believe God will be patient with you while you work on your faith?

Prayer Prompt

How long, Lord? Will you hide yourself forever?
    How long will your wrath burn like fire?
Remember how fleeting is my life.
    For what futility you have created all humanity!
Who can live and not see death,
    or who can escape the power of the grave?
Lord, where is your former great love. . . .

Praise be to the Lord forever!
Amen and Amen.
Psalm 89:46–49, 52

10
Navigating No-Man's-Land

Joseph's Story
No Good Deed

Based on Genesis 39

$\mathcal{T}$he first time it happens, Joseph thinks he has heard her wrong.

His master, Potiphar, has gone on a three-month journey, and Joseph plans to use the time to reorganize the entire household.

Joseph is going room to room, taking inventory of linens, lost in the work—the only way to keep thoughts of his family at bay. The harder he works, the less he remembers. So he doesn't hear her enter, doesn't sense her presence, until he catches a hint of jasmine, her fragrance. Startled, he looks up to find Potiphar's wife, Kiya, standing near, draped against a wall, long bronze legs peeking out from a slit in her gown.

"I'm sorry, ma'am," he says, "I didn't realize—" He moves toward the door.

"Come to bed with me," Kiya says in a husky voice.

Joseph's lips part. His thoughts tangle.

After a long pause, he says, "You want—you need—help—in your bedroom?"

Kiya tosses her dark hair back and laughs at the ceiling. "Oh yes, I need help in my bedroom."

He sidles along the wall, toward the door. Feels her eyes on him, raking up and down. Words tumble. "I'll send Cleo—to help—right away." He sprints through the house, the gardens, the stables. Slips into an empty stall, slides to his knees in trampled hay, the smell of horses in his nose. Sweating, shaking.

Potiphar is a good husband. Why would Kiya do this?

Unbidden, his father's voice echoes in his mind, as it always does in times of trouble: "Careful, son. Watch yourself."

One misstep—one misunderstanding, one accusation—and everything he has built here these past years, this life he has cobbled together from the wreckage of loss, will all collapse.

If there is something worse than slavery, Joseph doesn't want to know what it is. Slavery to a cruel master, maybe. To a lesser man than Potiphar. Hard labor in fields, maybe. The kind that steals a man's health and brings early death.

He shuts his eyes, breathing a prayer, calling for strength. Surely if he remains righteous, God will not let him down—surely Joseph has already borne enough.

From now on he will live on constant alert, looking over his shoulder, staying out of Kiya's way. Outfoxing the fox.

Three months later, he has dodged her advances a dozen times. He has tried explaining, reasoning—"How could I do such a wicked thing and sin against Potiphar, against *God*?" She only laughs, his every protest adding strength to her desire. But Potiphar returns tonight, and surely—*surely*—she will stop now.

The morning bell sounds. Joseph ties his sash and strides to the kitchens. In the corner he finds the new maid, twisting her small fingers into knots. Cleo has suggested her as a possible nanny for the children, but she will need testing, proving.

"You, girl—your name?"

She blinks and flinches like a startled animal. She is intimidated by his role as head of household. "M–Miri." Her skin takes on a greenish hue.

He gives an encouraging smile. "Today you accompany me. I will show you how this house runs."

She ducks her head and scurries to his side.

To himself, Joseph sighs, relieved. With Miri as his constant shadow, he will be safe from Kiya all day long. They whirl through the morning tasks, Joseph rattling off instructions, Miri scuttling silently behind. Gradually the morning cool burns away. Noon heat beats hard against the house. He takes Miri to Potiphar's rooms to check the new furniture, hoping it will earn one of his master's rare smiles. "Potiphar will be pleased, I think. When we finish here, you can—" A gurgle sounds behind him, and he turns.

Miri is not standing at his elbow; she is hunched in a corner of the room, vomiting into a potted plant.

Joseph sends her off to Cleo and hefts the pot, hurrying it out of the house, muttering. He rushes back to clean the spatter from the walls. It's not the kind of work Joseph should be doing, but there's no time to summon anyone else before the stain and stench sink in. He is bent over, scrubbing, when he catches it: a hint of jasmine.

His stomach tightens.

He springs to his feet. Kiya stands in the doorway, a predatory gleam in her eyes. Quietly, she closes the door and leans back against it, trapping her prey. She bends one knee, sliding her foot up the door; the slit in her gown parts, revealing ankle, knee, thigh.

His father's voice sounds the internal alarm: "Out, get out, get out, boy." Joseph swallows hard past a knot in his throat, his eyes skipping around the room, avoiding Kiya and her cursed leg, seeking escape. Hard midday sun slants in through a window, warming the room. Can he fit through the opening? Cold sweat trickles down his back.

Kiya slinks toward him, sultry, sinuous. Bronze bangles clank as she reaches one hand up to rest a finger against her painted lips— "Shhh"—and her other hand comes up to clutch his cloak. His throat fills with sand. She pulls him in, so close he feels her breath, hot and sweet on his face.

He jerks back, but her grip tightens, amusement sparking behind her kohl-rimmed eyes. With a yank and a twist, he wrenches free of the cloak—Kiya yelps her surprise—but Joseph is already launching himself out the window.

All afternoon he finds work in the stables, dread making his limbs heavy. He tries to pray, but the only word he finds is "Help." The same word he prayed all those long days rattling over desert roads, bound in the back of slave traders' wagons, weeping for the family he had lost.

He tries to push the memory back where it belongs, locked in the deepest chamber of his mind, but he is undone. The seal is broken, pain seeping out. His hands shake at their tasks.

When the dinner bell sounds, he keeps working, doing what he has always done here, channeling everything—grief, fear, rage, *whys* beyond counting—into this new life, working himself ragged, chasing sleep without dreams.

Cleo comes to him with food, worry adding lines to her already wrinkled face. "Potiphar will be home before nightfall," she says. "You should not be here when he returns. Kiya is humiliated, and she will blame you—she has your cloak. If you value your life, you must run."

Joseph chokes out a laugh, remembering Egyptian eyes weighing him, coins changing hands. The value of a Hebrew life. He shakes his head. "Run where?" His voice is strangled, harsh. "I have no friends in Egypt. If I run, they will only hunt me down, and death is certain."

Cleo catches his wrist. "You cannot defend yourself to Potiphar. If you accuse his wife. . ."

"I know," Joseph says, suddenly tired, so tired. All of it—*all* of it—catching up to him in one exhausting wave. "I can offer no defense."

He hears Potiphar and his guards coming before he sees them—heavy footfalls, angry voices, clanking chains. Slowly he steps outside into fading evening light, determined to hold Potiphar's gaze.

He expects the anger on Potiphar's face, but it is the hurt, the betrayal, that cuts him. Takes him back in time, just for a moment.

"I have high hopes for you, boy," Potiphar said, clapping a hand on Joseph's shoulder. "From this day on, I entrust my home, my family—everything—to your care." With all the servants and slaves watching, Potiphar held up a sash, woven in his family colors. Tied it himself around Joseph's waist, a sign of authority. And for a moment, Joseph was a boy again, beaming up at his father, slipping his shoulders into a coat of many colors.

Hours later the barred prison door clangs shut, and Joseph collapses on a filthy floor, still wearing Potiphar's sash. Too overwhelmed even to cry or protest or pray, he sits silent.

Prison.

Prison is what's worse than slavery.

My house was quiet. Too quiet. When a house with a kid in it sits silent for more than sixty seconds, something's up—usually something messy or dangerous.

So I went on a kid hunt. At last I found my four-year-old, crouched in a corner of her bedroom in her princess dress, up to her ears in jewels and tulle.

"What are you doing, sweetie? Is something wrong?"

She turned big brown eyes up at me and whispered, "I'm waiting for my prince to come."

"Ohh," I said. "I see. Well. . .I've totally been there." Smiling to myself, I tiptoed out, leaving her alone with her wait.

Sometimes we wait like my daughter did: hunched in a corner, life on pause. Postponing food, fun, everything. Just waiting.

And while we sit there, we think things like this:

I can't be happy unless. . .

I can't concentrate until. . .

I can't come out of hiding unless. . .

I won't be productive until. . .

I can't give my whole heart unless. . .

My only goal is to survive.

Raise your hand if you have thought these things during waiting seasons. (Me!)

Time Wasted, Life Lost

The temptation during waiting times is to do absolutely nothing. To sit around twiddling our thumbs, playing mind-numbing games on smartphones or absently scrolling through friends' Instagram pictures, envying the productive and meaningful lives everyone else seems to be leading, just biding our time. Waiting.

But unless we want to spend our entire waiting season living life on pause, hiding in the corner in our tiara and tulle, we have to work past the *untils* and *unlesses*. We have to live in spite of the *if onlys*. Now *if only* that were as easy as it sounds.

Confession: I sort of enjoy the waiting rooms at doctors' offices. For a few minutes, while I wait for my name to be called, I lose myself in magazines, finding out which celebrities have lost all their baby weight three days after childbirth and discovering what fashion trends I should have started wearing six months ago. It's brainless and stupid, a meaningless but fun way to spend the time.

For about fifteen minutes.

But then I start to get restless. I find myself repenting of mean thoughts toward celebrities and being overwhelmed by the "36 Ways to Pair Ankle Boots with Boyfriend Jeans." I'm ready to get out of the waiting room, have my appointment, move on with my real life. At this point, I start sneaking looks at all the other people in the waiting room, wondering if they're as bored as I am. Sometimes I'll spot someone with a computer on her lap, actually getting work done. I feel a stab of guilt: *I should have planned ahead. If I'd known I was going to be stuck waiting for so long, I would have brought some work along.*

If we are not careful, we spend our waiting seasons the same way we spend our time in waiting rooms: brainless, frivolous, unmotivated. Waiting seasons become time wasted, life lost. Waiting becomes our full-time occupation—our *only* occupation. We check out mentally and emotionally, disengage from the people we love, and kick into float-aimlessly-through-life-while-we-wait-for-something-to-change mode.

That's no way to live.

Because the thing is, we don't know how long we have to wait before our name gets called. It could be a long time. (Sorry, friend. Truly, I hope you don't have much longer to wait, but you just never know.) So in the meantime, as long as we are in the waiting room, we have decisions to make:

How will I wait?

How will I use this time?

Who do I want to be during this waiting season?
How can God use my life even now?

Joseph's Example

Joseph could be the Bible's poster child for waiting. Born into privilege, his father's favored son, "well-built and handsome" (Genesis 39:6), Joseph knows he is bound for greatness. In Joseph's youth, God gives him visions foretelling his success; he only has to wait to see them fulfilled. But then, one random afternoon, Joseph's Awesome Life Plan goes off the rails. (Ever felt that way? So sure your life is going in the right direction, going somewhere great, and then—*boom*—a major life curve changes everything.)

One day Joseph is a beloved son with a bright future; the next, a foreign slave with no rights. Sold by jealous older brothers into slavery, seventeen-year-old Joseph finds himself alone in another country, the slave of a wealthy and influential Egyptian, Potiphar, the captain of the guard.

I'm sorry, but if I were Joseph, I might have spent a few years moping around feeling sorry for myself. Questioning God, hating the world. Not Joseph. Even though he is surely heartbroken and homesick, still he gives his best efforts to his work as Potiphar's slave. Before long, he rises to become the trusted head of Potiphar's household, second only to Potiphar himself. For a while, things are as good as they can be—for a slave.

Unfortunately, Joseph's success (and appearance) brings him the unwanted attention of Potiphar's wife, who tries to seduce him. When Joseph refuses her advances, she accuses him of trying to rape her, and off to prison he goes.

Surely *now* Joseph will take a break from being awesome and just sit around sulking for the rest of his life, right? Surely this is the final insult, the one that kills his faith and breaks his spirit? No.

Again Joseph digs deep inside and somehow finds the courage, the faith, the will to keep living, and *living well*. His attitude and industry set him apart from everyone else, and before long Joseph becomes the prisoner in charge of all the other prisoners!

We don't know how long Joseph waits there in prison—it must be significantly longer than two years (Genesis 41:1)—but wait he does. In the meantime he serves and works in the prison. As far as he knows, he might be spending the rest of his life there.

The Thing We Can Control

There's no way Joseph is happy for even a second about being a slave or a prisoner. But there he is, and he has a choice: sit around feeling frustrated and unhappy, or get up and build a life *where he is in that moment.*

Build a life as a slave? Yep. That's what Joseph chooses to do. I wonder if he thinks to himself, *This is awful. But if I have to be a slave, then I'm going to be the best slave I can be.* Now that is an impressive attitude.

It doesn't get much worse than being a slave. . .unless you are a prisoner. And that's what happens to Joseph next.

Build a life as a prisoner? Yep. That's what Joseph chooses to do: *This is even more awful than slavery. But if I have to be a prisoner, then I'm going to be the best prisoner I can be.* Although our vignette stopped at Joseph's moment of crisis, we see in Genesis 39:21–23 that although Joseph is hurting, he chooses to work hard and make his life count, even in prison.

One of the most frustrating things about waiting seasons is feeling that we have no control over our situation. (And let's be honest: feeling out of control is pretty much the worst feeling ever for every woman on earth.) *In theory* we understand that we are never fully in control of our lives, but waiting seasons bring us face-to-face with our own humanity, our own limits. The longer we wait, the more helpless we feel.

But I have good news! We do control one thing even while we are waiting: we control *how we wait.* I'm not saying it will be easy, but we get a choice.

A choice in how we think.

A choice in how we feel.

A choice in how we act.

A choice in how we spend time.

A choice in who we become.

Joseph took charge of his life by taking charge of his attitude. You and I can make similar decisions on our waiting journeys even if we are winding through mile after mile of no-man's-land, no exit ramp in sight.

How Will I Use This Time?

Even as a prisoner and a slave, Joseph does great things with his time and talents. He doesn't waste the years. He grows as a person and develops skills that later prove invaluable. In fact, it is his excellence during the waiting times that ultimately gets him out of his painful predicament and prepares him to become Pharaoh's right-hand man. But it takes years. *Years.* As in *decades.*

So what about you and me? How can we use our in-between times? *Will* we use them? Or will we just coast along on cruise control, trying to survive? Trying not to think, not to engage, because it's just too painful?

Maybe instead of thinking of waiting journeys as time lost, time wasted, we can think of them as time *repurposed.* Time spent doing things we never would have gotten to do otherwise. We can use our waiting times as opportunities to develop new skills, try new things, go new places, enjoy unexpected detours and surprising scenery. No, those things might not be our first choice for this season of life, but they are still good choices and meaningful ways to spend time.

Friend, you can take charge of your time in the waiting room. Not in a way that says, "Forget You, God; You're doing a terrible job, so I'm taking the reins, doing things my way," but in a way that says, "Satan, you want to ruin this stage of my life, but I won't let you. I'm using this time for good and for God!"

Did you catch that last part? We can make God really, really, over-the-top happy by using waiting seasons for Him.

Jesus puts it this way: "Whoever wants to save their life will lose it, but whoever loses their life for me will save it" (Luke 9:24). Losing your life—giving yourself away, talents and time and heart and all—

will save you in the end. In fact, it will save you even now! Losing your life by choosing to serve others during a bleak time in your life, even when you feel you have little to give, will fill up your empty spaces. It will take the edge off your pain, show you the way out of loneliness, and make you feel whole again, even when something (or someone) is missing. No, it won't be exactly the same as if you had The Thing, but it will help.

Here's a funny irony: choosing self*less*ness instead of self*fish*ness is one of the best things we can do *for ourselves*! Why? Because the desire to have a job you love, a baby you love, a guy you love (who loves you back!)—those are all part of our God-given desire for meaning, purpose, love, and fulfillment. And giving helps us fill that God-given space. We are made to give.

And remember, Jesus says, "With the measure you use, it will be measured to you" (Luke 6:38). So how generous will you be right now? Give generously. God always, always, always outgives us in the end.

So you don't have The Thing right now. What *do* you have, and how can you give it away?

- Do you have more free time than you wish you had? How and where can you give time to others? To God?
- Even if you have not gotten the healing you seek, could your experience with illness, medication, or navigating a maze of medical options be helpful to others?
- Could your experience wrestling with mental illness— even if you are still struggling—be an encouragement to others suffering in similar ways?
- Do you have skills going unused and uncelebrated in your current job that could be a great help to your church or a local charity?
- Do you have an ocean of love inside, stored up for The Friend or The Guy or The Baby you don't yet have? Could someone else benefit from that love?
- Do you have underused talents or hobbies you could

share in some out-of-the-box way?

- Even as you wait, even as you hurt, do you see people around you needing comfort? People to whom *you* can be a friend?

My friend Rebecca, a retired teacher, is waiting to adopt a twelve-year-old boy. Every day he spends in a foster home is a day he spends apart from Rebecca and her husband and the forever home they long to give him. Every day apart, her heart aches for the time that can't be bought back. But you know what Rebecca is doing in the meantime? Pouring that love, saved up for a sweet boy, into a thirteen-year-old girl from our church who needs a friend. Rebecca goes to the girl's school once a week, sits through her classes, works with her teachers to help meet her unique educational needs, and serves as a liaison between the teachers and the girl's parents. Rebecca does this to help the girl (the girl just got straight As for the first time ever!), but the time they spend together also fills a part of the twelve-year-old-boy-shaped hole in Rebecca's heart. She gives comfort, but she also receives it.

I remember someone advising me, during our long baby-wait, to try to fill the emptiness in my heart by loving other people's kids. By spending time with my friends' children and showering them with love and attention. By volunteering in the kids' classes at church. The thing is, I adore kids, and theoretically, it was good advice, righteous advice, but at that point in my journey I was just too wounded. Spending time around other people's children just reinforced my own childlessness. Every time I saw a baby, I was gutted.

But do you know what I found I could do? I could give my free evenings to the college girls in our church's campus ministry; I could give away all the unspent love in my heart as an older sister and friend to girls a few years younger than I was. So that's what I did. That's how I spent my free time, where I poured out my maternal instincts. No, it wasn't the same thing as having a baby—not even remotely the same thing (no poopy diapers, but much more boyfriend drama)—but it was fun, it was fulfilling, and it made a difference. (Also, I got a puppy, and poured *waaaaaay* too much energy into training and shaping that poor dog's schedule. But that's another story, a kind of embarrassing story.)

Although many of my memories of our babyless years are painful ones, the memories with Laura and Jenni and Lauren and Amanda and Aimee and Nikki and many others sparkle as bright lights in dark times. On the day Kevin and I finally got to say those blessed words, *We are pregnant*, those girls mobbed me, screaming: "We—*aaahhh!*—food—years—*aaahhh!*—Wednesdays—*aaahhh!*" It took about ten minutes for me to finally untangle the words they were all shrieking at once: they'd been fasting and praying for me *every Wednesday for more than a year*, and they'd vowed never to tell me until the day I got pregnant. It was an astounding gift, one of the greatest of my life. To this day those girls—now women—remain friends, some now raising babies of their own.

Little by Little

Let's get back to Joseph's story. God rewards Joseph's nobility: "While Joseph was there in the prison, the LORD was with him; he showed him kindness and granted him favor in the eyes of the prison warden" (Genesis 39:20–21).

Fascinating, right? Joseph is waiting for relief. In his mind, relief probably looks like this: Joseph gets set free from slavery, sent home to his family. His brothers grovel and repent. His father showers him with gifts; his mother dotes on him. The dreams of his youth, the ones where he rules his family, are fulfilled.

But for many, many years, Joseph doesn't get the kind of relief he wanted—not even close. But even so, God is with him. In fact, God is *blessing Joseph*, even while Joseph suffers. Yep, you read that right: God is blessing Joseph even while He leaves him in slavery. Even while He leaves him in prison. Even while He lets him endure loneliness. Sure, Joseph would have preferred that God bless him by busting him out of prison and sending him home to his parents—but hey, sometimes we get a different kind of blessing.

I love this insight from Exodus, when God tells His people

(Joseph's descendants!) how He plans to give them the land He promised:

> *"I will send the hornet ahead of you to drive the Hi-*
> *vites, Canaanites and Hittites out of your way. But*
> *I will not drive them out in a single year, because the*
> *land would become desolate and the wild animals too*
> *numerous for you. Little by little I will drive them out*
> *before you, until you have increased enough to take*
> *possession of the land."*
>
> Exodus 23:28–30

Interesting, right? Sometimes God blesses His people little by little. We'd rather receive our blessings all at once, in one overwhelming windfall, but God says, *"Nope. Getting it all at once would hurt you more than help you. I'm going to give it to you gradually, to give you time to grow into the responsibility."*

Take a look at your life: Is God blessing you little by little, even now? Giving you pieces of what you have prayed for, in small increments? Why not stop to notice and savor small blessings along the way? God might not be rescuing you from the waiting, but perhaps He is blessing you in other ways, filling your life with other joys. Pray to have an attitude that God *can* bless and eyes to see the blessings He is already giving—even if they look different than the blessings you are praying for.

Who Will You Become?

Here's another way to take back control as we navigate the waiting wilderness: Let's decide who we want to be during this time. We don't get to choose what happens *to* us, but we get to choose what happens *in* us. We choose *who we become*.

We can choose bitterness, or gratitude.

We can choose selfishness, or selflessness.

We can choose inertia, or productivity.

We can let this time frustrate us, or fuel us.

Remember Jesus' parable of the ten virgins (Matthew 25:1–13)? The ten bridesmaids wait with the bride for her groom to arrive, and those who think and plan ahead are ready when the groom comes. Those who are thoughtless miss out on the fun. When your waiting season ends—and chances are, it will end all of a sudden, when you least expect it—will you be ready for the party or caught off guard?

And remember Jesus' parable of the talents (Matthew 25:14–30)? The master is gone for an unspecified time, and he is proud of servants who use the time productively. God calls us to live with purpose, even during in-between times. To be ready for action when it's time to act.

If you choose to grow in even one character trait—faith, confidence, selflessness—during your waiting season, then your suffering has not been wasted. How can you grow, how can you change, how can you become a better, stronger you?

James 4:8 encourages us, "Come near to God and he will come near to you." When we take a step in a spiritual direction, God takes a step, too—in *our* direction. When we make godly choices, God is right there, cheering us on and giving us strength. We are not alone.

Time out for a reality check. Look, we are not going to do this waiting thing perfectly. We are going to have months when we mope, weeks when we twiddle our thumbs, and days when getting out of bed is the best we can do. And you know what? That's fine. I'm not trying to guilt-trip you, because honestly, sometimes I have felt like the world's worst waiter. I think God laughed really hard at me when He decided He wanted me to write this book. I have fallen flat on my face and then lain there throwing a tantrum a shameful number of times. But. . .*but*. I'd be remiss if I did not call us higher. Give us things to shoot for during these times. Call us to dig deep and find our best selves, even through heartache. Our waiting will be messy sometimes, ugly sometimes, but if we just keep fighting, we can reclaim this time. It need not be time lost. Okay, time in.

Mr. Letterman Jacket's Story

Have you ever had one of those times when everything is going grandly—life is just sing-in-the-car-with-the-windows-down-and-then-run-through-a-field-of-flowers wonderful—and then *bam*, you are running through flowers, singing, and you get mauled by a wolf hiding in the grass?

That's what happened to Mr. Letterman Jacket when we first started dating.

Kevin had finally (finally!) gotten the heavenly message through his thick skull that I was the woman of his dreams (the memo involved Kevin ~~spying on me~~ spotting me taking a bite of a candied apple while on a date with another boy in Paris, because two can play the go-out-with-other-people-in-Paris game), and a few weeks later we started dating. (My Doc Martens did not touch ground for a month.) That same week, he started two-a-day summer practices for football, which is basically when coaches try to kill their players before the season starts. The players who survive are counted worthy to play come fall. Our school's longtime quarterback had just graduated, and it was time for a new guy to take over. Kevin was the next-oldest quarterback, next in line, so he had worked his tail off getting ready. He had spent the last two summer breaks at school, working out with the players who were in town. He had memorized the playbook, developed great relationships with his teammates, even added ten pounds of muscle (I *might* have noticed, especially when we went to see scary movies and he "accidentally" flexed every time I grabbed his arm).

Kevin had spent three years waiting his turn, studying the game, working hard, supporting the quarterback ahead of him. Now it was his time, his turn, and he wasn't going to squander it.

So he showed up to that first two-a-day practice ready to give, ready to lead, ready to (literally) take the ball. Instead, before practice even started, the coach said, "Kevin, I've decided to work with the younger quarterbacks instead of you. You go over and practice with the scout team."

What's the scout team, you ask? (I know, this is a girl's book. Some of you do not speak Football—I only speak it because of Kevin.) Scout team is the practice team, the guys who don't expect to see playing time. They are there to get beat up on by the first- and second-team players. (Ever seen the movie *Rudy*? Rudy played on the scout team.) Most are walk-on players, not even on scholarship.

Just like that, all of Kevin's work was for nothing. Just like that, the dream He had been working for since he was nine went up in smoke. He never even took a single snap in two-a-days. Never got a chance.

When Kevin called me that night, I could hear the anguish in his voice: he hadn't just been passed over; he had been humiliated. Sucker punched. Betrayed. (Later, when Kevin asked his coach for an explanation, the coach said, "You're two inches too short. I like my quarterbacks to be six four.")

Kevin could have become bitter. Could have let the injustice destroy him. Could have become one of the gazillion embittered football players in the world with a sob story about how their coach did them wrong, how no one believed in them and saw how awesome they were, yada yada.

Kevin refused to do that. He cried and prayed and prayed and cried some more. He went out to the school gardens and wandered, wrestling with God for hours. I sat and listened and cried with him and prayed with him.

And then he decided that if he was going to be on the scout team, he was going to make it the best scout team in Division I football. He was going to make the whole team better by pushing the worst guys on the team to be their best. And that's what he did. All season long, he led the scout team as if they were competing for the national championship.

All season long, I watched from the stands as Kevin stood on the sidelines calling in plays for the other quarterbacks, helping them warm up, and giving them butt slaps when they ran on and off the field. (Again, if you don't speak Football, let me interpret: The butt slap is a flexible and nuanced gesture, rich with masculine meaning. It can mean everything from "You got this, bro" to "Great play" to "That stunk, but I love you anyway.") No one cheered harder, encouraged more, or *led* more on that team than Kevin—Kevin, the third-string quarterback, the "extra" one.

If the coaches noticed, they never said anything. Never recognized his servant leadership. It was one of the most striking cases of in-your-face unfairness either of us had ever experienced in our young lives.

But you know who did notice?

I did. Kevin's team did. Our friends did. Most importantly, *God did.*

Kevin's example inspired many and laid the groundwork for the man he has become. Even now I see the humility, self-sacrifice, God-reliance, and resilience he developed during that time, still at work in the man he is and the work he does. (See chapter 12 to read the rest of Kevin's football story.)

Big Decisions in In-Between Times

When I was fifteen, my family moved unexpectedly from Miami to New Jersey. The three years we lived in Miami had not been the happiest time for me. A few things had been great—we lived near my beloved grandparents, my parents enjoyed their work, my siblings were happy, I became a Christian—but overall, my own years there were riddled with insecurity and loneliness.

But I remember that long road trip up to New Jersey in our ancient white-with-wood-trim Dodge Caravan, gazing out at the breathtaking beauty of fog hovering over the Shenandoah Valley, having an epic, ponderous teenage-girl moment. (Cue smarmy rock ballad here, preferably something by Journey.) I thought about the girl I had been in Miami—insecure, self-centered, isolated—and decided that I didn't want to be that girl anymore.

New Jersey was a new place, and for me it would be a new start. I asked God to help me change, to become more outgoing, more joyful, more open to friendship. And I decided that no matter what my new school was like, I would be different. I would stand tall, look people in the eye, risk giving my heart even when I was scared, and see the best in whatever and whomever I met "up north."

And you know what? Things were different—*I* was different—from the moment that Caravan door opened on New Jersey soil. A new day, a new and happier time in my life, had begun. I look back on that minivan moment as a turning point in my teenage years: a moment in-between, when I became more of the girl God meant me to be.

It felt as if God met me halfway: I made a decision in my heart, and then He stepped in and paved the way for the change to happen. Within a week, I'd already met two people who became dear friends. Twenty-five years later, we are still friends, all because of a prayer on a road trip: A suspended moment in time when life was on pause. A place between stops, a leg of the journey, a moment of clarity when God came down and helped me change.

Don't underestimate the power of decisions you make in the middle of your journey, in the places between. Maybe you feel like you're on an endless road trip right now, to places uncharted, a future unknown. The road stretches on past the horizon, unmarked and seemingly endless, curves without end.

Like Joseph, we all get to choose how we navigate no-man's-land. We may yet be long miles from the place where we want to end up, but we can redeem the time. When the trip ends and the car door opens at last onto new soil, we will smile as we set foot in a new place. We might stretch unused muscles and kiss the ground, relieved to be free from the cramped car, but let's hope we can look back on those road-trip hours with some happy memories, knowing we are stronger now than we were at the start.

Let's take back this time.

Let's use it for God instead of letting it go to waste.

Let's give what we have as we wait for what we want.

Let's not waste the wait.

Waiting Room Reading

For Further Study
Joseph's story is found in Genesis 37–50.

Journal Prompt
1.   How can you glorify God with your life during this time? Can

you think of some unique ways you can serve Him while you wait?

2. Who do you want to be and become during this time? (Think about words like *peaceful, grateful, kind, selfless, faithful, positive, prayerful, serving, mature, active, productive, open, honest, strong, realistic, fun.*) What scriptures can help you develop those strengths?

Prayer Prompt

I will sing of your love and justice, LORD.
I will praise you with songs.
I will be careful to live a blameless life—
when will you come to help me?
I will lead a life of integrity
in my own home.
I will refuse to look at
anything vile and vulgar.
I hate all who deal crookedly;
I will have nothing to do with them.
I will reject perverse ideas
and stay away from every evil.
I will not tolerate people who slander their neighbors.
I will not endure conceit and pride.

PSALM 101:1–5 NLT

11
Gifts Waiting Gives Us

Martha's Story
Joy in the Mourning

Based on John 11:1–44

*H*sss, hsss.

Back and forth, a relentless saw. Martha tries to say, "Stop," but her tongue is glued to the roof of her mouth.

Hsss, hsss.

It hurts, the sound. They're cutting her heart from her chest.

Eyes flying open, Martha jerks awake. Pushes up onto elbows, cradling her aching head in her hands. She blinks: dark room, hard chair, small bed. She is tipping out of the chair, half draped across the foot of the bed.

Hsss, hsss. She follows the sound.

Lazarus. Her body spasms with sudden memory: the lingering illness, the terrible turn. Her brother lies sallow on sheets, eyes shut, searching for air, fighting his lungs.

She leaps to her feet, puts a palm to his forehead: hot, so hot. Counting heartbeats: slow—*please, no*—far too slow. She watches his chest struggling to rise, pausing too long.

Please, God, no. No no no.

She sprints from the room. "Mary! *Mary!*"

Her sister's tousled head pokes through a doorway, eyes puffy and confused, braid falling loose over one shoulder.

"I—I fell asleep, I was supposed to keep watch. He turned. . .I "
Martha's thoughts splinter. She flaps her hands, helpless birds.

Mary, trembling, looks up at her, a tableau of grief: hands cupped over her mouth, big brown eyes brimming with tears.

They stand before their parents' newly sealed tomb, the
last to leave. A family of five suddenly reduced to three.
Lazarus stands beside Martha, his boy shoulders held
soldier-straight, red eyes tearless because now he is the
man, the protector—but somehow his hand finds Mar-
tha's. Squeezes. Lends what courage he has. She forces
her own shoulders back, wrestles back the tide of tears:
she, too, must be strong. Strong like Mother. Strong like
Lazarus. Strong for Mary.

    She reaches for her sister's hand, but it's not there.
Mary kneels in dirt, braids swinging, tiny hands
pressed against her mouth, trying—failing—to hold
back the sound. Sobs tear free—brutal, broken—and all
Martha can think is, This is what it sounds like when
childhood dies. *She kneels to gather her sister in her*
arms. "Shhh." Seconds later Lazarus's arms close around
Martha from behind, wrapping both sisters. His arms,
still growing, somehow big enough, strong enough.

Martha bangs a fist against her forehead, wills herself calm. *Think. Plan.* "Mary, I'll take care of everything. You go sit with Lazarus, I'll. . ."—everything stops, just for a moment, dust motes dance in dawn light—"Jesus! I'll send for Jesus! He's nearby—He's back in Jerusalem!"

Mary's eyes widen, hope sparkling through tears. "Jesus!" she breathes, throwing her arms around Martha, speaking muffled words into her shoulder. "Of course. Jesus will come. Jesus loves him. Jesus will heal him."

For a moment, Martha sags into the hug, borrows faith. *Hurry.* Blinking hard, she pushes back, keeping both hands on Mary's petite shoulders. "Yes. Of course He will. There is still time." She pulls Mary in for one more quick, firm hug. "Now go: keep watch, keep him comfortable." Mary flashes a smile, candle in darkness, and hurries away. Martha sees hope in her sister's footsteps, and it turns her inside out. *Jesus must come. Lazarus must live. Mary must keep smiling.*

She turns on her heel, whipping her hair into a bun, whirling into motion.

"Matthew! I need you!" Her brain churns out a list of everything she might need to keep Lazarus breathing—*water, thread, pot, cloth.* She starts tossing things onto a tray. *Where is that boy?* "Matthew! *Now!*"

A gangly servant boy skids into the room, panting, fumbling with a sash around his waist. His hair sticks out sideways. Any other day she would laugh, tease him, make him wet it down. "Yes, ma'am?"

"Run to Jerusalem, find Jesus—you remember our rabbi friend? Of course you remember; none could forget. Tell Him, 'Lord, the one you love is sick.' Stop for nothing, run as fast as you can. Lazarus's life depends on it."

Matthew nods once, serious and slow, accepting the weight of his mission, a man's life in his hands—*shoulders back, a man too soon, just like Lazarus all those years ago*—and dashes for the door.

For a moment, Martha stands paralyzed, throat throbbing. Unsaid words, unshed tears. *My life depends on it, too.* Prayer takes wing, a wordless cry.

She shakes herself into movement. *Water, thread, pot, cloth.* Keep moving, slow time. Just a few hours—surely Lazarus will only have to hold on for a few hours before help arrives.

By nightfall Jesus will be here.

By nightfall everything will be okay.

Days later. . .

Martha gazes tearlessly on her family's tomb, listening to Mary's cries. Between sisters, where Lazarus should be, stands Jesus.

Mary's pain has found fresh force now their friend has finally arrived. Days of weeping have left her wails raw, her voice ragged. Though Mary's every cry draws fresh blood, it's an internal bleed.

A small gasp, a hiss of breath—not Mary's. Martha turns. Her lips part in surprise: Jesus, shoulders hunched, is shaking with tears. He looks up, meets her eyes, offers a watery smile. She waits for Him to turn away, wipe His eyes, hide His grief, but instead He reaches out and puts one gentle, brotherly arm around Martha, the other around Mary.

Just as Lazarus would have done.

He is standing in.

The tenderness tears something loose, gives Martha's sorrow a voice.

Jesus lets the sisters cry till they're spent, one on each shoulder: bearing their grief, adding tears of His own.

At last He hands Mary off to Martha and steps forward. Rolling up His sleeves and clearing His throat, He turns to the crowd of mourners. His eyes are red, His gaze determined. "Take away the stone!"

Shocked into action, Martha steps forward. She speaks low, the relatives' eyes heavy on her: "Lord, I know You want to say Your good-byes, but it has been four days, and by now"—she hesitates, thinking, *Why must I always be the practical one?*—"there will be an odor."

Jesus gives her a half smile. "Martha, Martha," He whispers. "Didn't I tell you that you would see the glory of God? Won't you trust Me?"

Palms up, she breathes an I-hope-you-know-what-you're-doing sigh and steps back to her sister.

When the stone has been moved, Jesus looks up and says a prayer. Draws a deep breath and shuts His eyes. Shouts, "Lazarus! Come out!"

Jesus turns to Martha, a grin just for her.

Time stops.

Mary gasps in Martha's arms.

In the darkness of the tomb, *something moves.*

Waiting precedes miracles.

Sometimes waiting *forces* miracles. But a miracle is not a miracle without a wait.

When Jesus heard Lazarus was sick, *He waited on purpose*. Even knowing the dire need, knowing death was coming, Jesus still stayed away, because He had a plan.

> *Now a man named Lazarus was sick. He was from Bethany, the village of Mary and her sister Martha. (This Mary, whose brother Lazarus now lay sick, was the same one who poured perfume on the Lord and wiped his feet with her hair.) So the sisters sent word to Jesus, "Lord, the one you love is sick."*
>
> *When he heard this, Jesus said, "This sickness will not end in death. No, it is for God's glory so that God's Son may be glorified through it." Now Jesus loved Martha and her sister and Lazarus. So when he heard that Lazarus was sick, he stayed where he was two more days.*
>
> JOHN 11:1–6

Did you catch that nuance there in the last part? "Jesus loved Martha and her sister and Lazarus. *So. . .he stayed.*" *So* means *because*. Jesus waited because He loved them. Because He had something astounding up His sleeve. A gift: a transcendent moment with Jesus, their friend and Lord. Front-row seats—more, supporting roles—in this, perhaps His most dramatic and deliberate miracle.

If Martha and Mary had gotten an immediate answer when they begged for help, they would have gotten a healing, but not a resurrection. They wouldn't have experienced this, their family's greatest and most intimate miracle.

Every wait doesn't get a miracle, but some do.

Some of mine certainly have, and they are the greatest treasures of my life, my shining moments with God. His arms around me there at the tomb, staving off death.

But here's the other thing, a crucial truth: Even when we don't receive the miracle of *yes*—the last-minute save, the brother walking out of a tomb—we still receive *other miracles* through waiting. Smaller, subtler miracles. They might not have fireworks and fanfare, but they are miracles nonetheless.

The smallest diamond is still a jewel.

Waiting Lets People Love You

When our family moved to North Carolina five years ago, we limped into town, emotionally shattered. In an unexpected whirlwind of change and loss, we had left our parents, our friends, our life, all while I was still bleeding from a miscarriage. We had suffered so many *nos* from God in a month, I could hardly eat. (When you spend days bleeding on a couch, binge-watching the entire *Lord of the Rings* extended-version series and every available season of *Castle* because you can't bear the real world, it's bad. It's very, very bad.)

A week after our arrival in North Carolina, I was invited to take fifteen minutes to introduce myself to the congregation where we would be serving for a short time. I wasn't ready. It was too soon. I was still bleeding. I could hardly stand for fifteen minutes without getting dizzy. I almost said no, I needed more time.

But after praying about it, I decided I needed to speak. The women might not meet like this, all together, for another six months, and by then we'd be packing to move again, so it was now or never.

There would be no pretending. I didn't have energy or emotional reserve to stand up there all happy-happy and charming. I decided to tell the church, these hundreds of women, exactly where we were and how we had come to them. So I stood, dizzy and shaking, and told our story—yes, all the good God had done for us over the years, but all we had recently lost. I cried. I felt vulnerable, naked. A little embarrassed.

When I sat down, I was swarmed by women offering hugs, tears, and sympathy, their own stories of miscarriage and loss.

The next day, dinners started showing up at my house from people I had never met—some of whom I *never met*. The women in that blessed church didn't let me cook for a month. They just gave us food and gave me time. The time we needed to heal. I am forever grateful.

Even when you don't get the miraculous *yes*, you may receive love.

Support. Prayer. Encouragement. Comfort. Maybe a pie or two. And these are no small gifts.

Let's back up fifteen years. It's my sophomore year in college, at my dream school, and all my thoughts are consumed with Shakespeare, sharing my faith, and a certain boy in a letterman jacket who keeps showing up to eat breakfast in my dining hall. (Coincidence? Surely not. No stinking way. He has to be doing this on purpose. If a girl "accidentally" shows up to eat with a boy she likes every other day, it's premeditated, it means something—*please, God, let this mean something.*)

One spring afternoon, I'm sitting in my dorm room and the phone rings.

"Hi, sweetie, it's Dad."

Dad and I are very close, but in those days he rarely calls; he is not really a phone person. Suspicion rises.

"Honey, I need to tell you something."

Worst-Case Scenario Disorder kicks in immediately: somebody's sick, somebody has cancer. *Please, God, not my baby sister.* My heart starts jackhammering in my chest.

"It's about school."

School? What's wrong with school? I just made assistant editor at the paper, I'm dorm president, my GPA is great. I'm in love with a boy who keeps maybe accidentally maybe on purpose showing up to eat breakfast with me. . . School is *amazing.* In fact, I never want to graduate.

"I can't pay for it anymore."

Silence. I'm so shocked, I can't even sputter.

"Honey, I'm so sorry. I thought we could do it—we've tried so hard." The words tumble together, words like *equity, irresponsible,* and *three other kids.*

I force a brave voice. "Okay, Dad. I know you tried."

When we hang up, I'm too stunned even to cry. I can't tell Dad what I'm really thinking: Never once in my life have I gotten to finish a school I started. Two elementary schools, three middle schools, three high schools. I always have to leave. It's happening again.

For the first time, I look around my school and notice all the BMWs and the J.Crew plaid, and realize *I didn't grow up the way most of these people did. I love them, I'm friends with them, but I don't have what they have.*

A few days later, Dad calls back. "Sweetie, I don't want to get your hopes up, but some of my friends want to help us figure this out. I'm just telling you so you can pray."

There is nothing I can do *but* pray.

It's a little embarrassing, but while Dad does the father thing, I start asking close friends to pray. My entire campus ministry starts praying. I take long walks around the school I love, begging my Father for a miracle. I even make a secret vow: "God, if You do this for me, I will never stop telling people the story."

A few weeks later, a two-thousand-dollar check arrives, a "scholarship" from one of Dad's friends. This is no scholarship. It is kindness. We swallow hard—Dad didn't ask for this—but we accept it with thanks. It's still just a drop in the seventy-thousand-dollar bucket, but it's a start.

And then Dad calls with an update: Another friend, Art, has a friend, a vice president at a national bank. This man has never met me—never even met my dad—but he is a friend of Art's, and any friend of Art's is apparently a friend of Dad's. A friend of mine.

Several weeks later, Dad calls again: "Meet me in the financial aid office tomorrow." At the appointed time, I throw on my most responsible outfit and dash across campus. A secretary ushers me into the office of the dean of financial aid, where I sit in a chair and try not to giggle in nervous amazement at the sight of three men squeezed onto a single couch: Dad, Art, and Mr. Bank Vice President, whom I have just met for the first time. The dean is smiling this baffled smile and throwing me sideways searching glances, like, *Who is this young lady, that all these men come running to defend her?* I give him a baffled grin in return: *I'm nobody—just a daughter of Sam and a daughter of God!*

I sit there nodding, doing my best to look worthy and super responsible as four men throw around numbers and words, as Mr. Bank

Vice President waves papers, breaks down my parents' finances, and finally declares, "The burden is too much for this family."

Half an hour later, we all stand and shake hands. The dean walks us out, promising, "I'll take a look and call you in a week."

A week.

Seven long days to wait and pray.

We pray our guts out.

A week later, I'm with my family. The phone rings and Dad passes it to me, eyebrows raised.

It's the dean.

Calling *me*.

"Hi, Elizabeth. I looked over your family's finances, and it seems we've made some mistakes in your financial aid these past two years. I'd like to set things right."

He pauses.

The longest two seconds in the world, my fate in his hands.

"How does eighteen thousand dollars a year sound for the next two years? Could you stay in school if we gave you that?"

I cover the phone, whisper the number to Dad, and watch his eyeballs nearly pop out of their sockets. I take that as a yes.

My heart threatens to rocket out of my chest. I try to sound cool, calm. Like I'm not freaking out, even as Dad is whispering to Mom, and they're both waving their arms around like adorable little weirdos. "Why yes, sir, I think eighteen thousand dollars a year might just do the trick."

We hang up.

I'm pretty sure the whole state hears our screams.

Every other month for the rest of my college career, I drop by the dean's office. Every time, he stops whatever he is doing and invites me to sit with him, even though I'm nobody. I tell him how school is going, how happy I am. Eventually I tell him about how Mr. Letterman Jacket has declared his undying love and sold his trumpet to buy me a ring.

I will never forget the gift those men gave me—my father's friends. Never had I felt so loved by God's church, so cared for by

God's people. So loved by my two dads: my earthly dad and my heavenly one.

And these words are me, fulfilling my Hannah prayer, my promise to God, telling the world what God did—through the kindness of friends—for a twenty-year-old girl all those years ago. *"Come and hear, all you who fear God; let me tell you what he has done for me"* (Psalm 66:16).

When you wait, if you dare to share your struggles with friends—even when they are embarrassing, even when you'd rather keep them to yourself—you open yourself up to receive care and kindness. You find out how much people love you, how much they have to give. You find goodness in unexpected places.

Waiting Lets You Be a Friend to Others

> *Thank God, the Father of our Lord Jesus Christ, that he is our Father and the source of all mercy and comfort. For he gives us comfort in our trials so that we in turn may be able to give the same sort of strong sympathy to others in theirs. Indeed, experience shows that the more we share Christ's suffering the more we are able to give of his encouragement. This means that if we experience trouble we can pass on to you comfort and spiritual help; for if we ourselves have been comforted we know how to encourage you to endure patiently the same sort of troubles that we have ourselves endured. We are quite confident that if you have to suffer troubles as we have done, then, like us, you will find the comfort and encouragement of God.*
>
> 2 CORINTHIANS 1:3–7 PHILLIPS

Want to know one of the amazing blessings you might experience as a result of your waiting seasons? The ability to comfort others who are going through a similar trial. The ability to sympathize—and strongly. The wisdom to pass along the comfort God Himself has given you.

Even as you wait, even as you hurt, do you see people around you needing comfort? People to whom you can be a friend?

Infertility doesn't bring many joys into your life, but for me it has brought one great blessing: friendship. Over the years, I have connected with women all over the world who have reached out because they heard I once endured a season of infertility. They are friends of friends, and I count it a privilege to pray with them, hurt with them, laugh together at the horrific humor found in things like sperm baths and ultrasound wands. (You don't want to know, friend; oh, I pray you never have to know.) Every time I connect with a new friend enduring the agony of a baby-wait, I think: *This is God redeeming lost time. Bringing good from misery, wringing joy from despair. Those awful fruitless years are even now bearing fruit.*

How can your story help others? The more open you are about your own struggles, the more you will be able to minister to others when the time is right. You may not be ready now, but maybe one day, when you are traveling a more peaceful leg of your journey, you'll find words to share. Stories to tell. Comfort to pass on. You will look back with a jolt of joy and think, *God is using my loss for good. He is "Romans 8:28-ing" on me, just like He promised!*

Spiritual Growth (a.k.a. The Part Where I Eat My Words)

It might not sound glamorous, but spiritual growth is no small gift. Waiting forges things in our hearts that cannot be wrought any other way.

Humility, compassion, patience, depth, strength, empathy—these are just a few of the characteristics waiting has cultivated in me. Do I now look back on the season I spent longing for true love, feeling lost and alone, and think, *Wow, I'm so happy I waited so long for Kevin?* Sort of. Not exactly, but kind of yes. During those years, I learned to walk closely with God, to let *Him* hold my hand and give me confidence.

Do I look back on the years Kevin and I spent begging God to give us children, and think, *Oh, I'm so happy we walked through hell on earth. I'm so glad all my friends had babies before me. I'm thrilled that I spent thousands of dollars on humiliating doctor visits while friends got pregnant for free by forgetting to take their birth control pills?* No, I don't. Can I say that *everything* that came from those years was good? No, I can't.

But I can say that I am deeply thankful for the person I became because of those years, that suffering. I stand forever changed. Waiting has transformed everything: how I look at God, how I pray, how I read the Bible, how I view myself, how I relate to my husband, what I expect from life, how I minister to hurting people, how I parent the children God finally blessed me with. For *those* things—those gifts—I am thankful. You couldn't pay me ten million dollars to relive the excruciating baby-wait years, but I *am* grateful for the good they brought later.

I recognize that I am still processing my waiting seasons, discovering life lessons. Still growing, still changing, still striving to become "mature and complete" (again our old friend, James 1:4).

So what can we learn? Who can we become? Who *are we becoming* even today, smack in the middle of the wait?

Learning and *becoming* might not sound like fun enterprises. Even if they aren't always fun, they are fulfilling. Rewarding. Growth is how we partner with God to make life count, give time purpose. We are not just twiddling our thumbs, waiting for something to happen. While we wait, we are *actively becoming* the people God wants us to be, people we will be proud to be at the end of our days.

Let's get practical. What are you most struggling with while you are waiting?

- Simple impatience?
- Discouragement?
- Self-pity?
- Resentment?
- Envy?
- Embarrassment?
- A feeling of inadequacy, compared to friends who already have what you want?
- Questioning God's love?

- Questioning God's *ability* to change your situation?
- All of the above? (And don't flip out if you are. I have certainly struggled—ahem, I am still struggling—with every one of these on some level, sometimes all at once!)

The temptations and questions we wrestle with show us where we can grow. Don't pressure yourself to master All the Things all at once; just pray about them and start addressing them one by one, little by little. Let the Bible guide your thoughts, your heart. Open up to godly friends about your struggle.

The 20/20 Myth

People say hindsight is 20/20.

I'm not so sure.

That statement implies that when we look back on our lives and on the journey it took to get us here (wherever *here* is), we should always be able to say, "Now I get it! I see the Grand Plan! I understand *exactly why* I had to go through (fill in the blank), and I'm just tickled pink about the whole experience. It all makes sense."

And you know, sometimes we do say that.

Every once in a while, we get one of those spine-tingling Aha Moments from God, when we see, for one sparkling, breath-stealing moment, all the disconnected pieces of life click into place: *this* needed to happen, at *this* exact time, so that *this* could happen. Oh, the beauty! In that shimmering space, God's genius stops time. The pieces fit; we catch a glimpse of one corner of the puzzle of life as it's being assembled. The clues come together: the plot twist, explained; the hero, unmasked! End credits roll and the audience stands and cheers.

But that kind of clarity doesn't happen as often as we'd like. When I look back on my life so far, hindsight is still foggy. Some things make sense; others leave me scratching my head: *Why did I go through that? Why did I wait so long?* I can't see the big picture, only parts. We *all* have puzzle pieces in life that don't seem to fit. Random plotlines that feel like tangents. Detours to apparent dead ends. We don't see all the things God can see, partly because we are not God and partly because our stories aren't finished.

And you know, I don't think we are *supposed* to look back on our lives and have everything figured out. Isn't omniscience God's job, not ours?

Looking back on my season of unrequited love, I can now appreciate the fact that Kevin and I both needed to grow up a lot before we were ready to start dating. . .so I confess I am glad we didn't make a mess of things by dating too soon. (But here's the thing: if grown-up Elizabeth traveled back in time and *said* that to in-love-in-college Elizabeth, in-love-in-college Elizabeth would probably kick grown-up Elizabeth in the head.)

If God drew us a map of our lives' journeys, tracking all our detours and delays, most of our maps would be a mess. (I think mine would look like a preschooler scribbled all over the Eastern United States at random, though I like to think there would also be lots of smiley faces scrawled along the edges.) Our maps would probably show long years spent wandering, circling back, meandering some more, repeating paths, hitting dead ends, offroading, getting stuck, ditching the car and hiking for a while. . .because life is messy.

Life rarely takes the most direct, time-efficient route.

Life isn't a movie script, written to be resolved in two hours with a satisfying happy ending and no loose ends.

Life is long. Life is surprising. Life is confusing.

Sometimes life takes us places we don't want to go: sickbeds, crosses, tombs.

Sometimes God stands outside the tomb and holds us while we cry. Mingles His tears with ours.

And sometimes—oh glorious day—He flashes a grin, rolls up His sleeves, and wakes up the dead.

Waiting Room Reading

For Further Study
You can read more about Martha and her siblings in Luke 10:38–42 and John 11:1–44; 12:1–3.

Journal Prompt

1. What gifts have you already received from waiting? Have you experienced any miracles or received special care from God or His people?
2. How can this time help you to become. . .
    more like Jesus?
    more faithful?
    more humble?
    more patient?
    more grateful?
    more compassionate?

Prayer Prompt

When You did awesome works
that we did not expect,
You came down,
and the mountains quaked at Your presence.
From ancient times no one has heard,
no one has listened,
no eye has seen any God except You,
who acts on behalf of the one who waits for Him.
ISAIAH 64:3–4 HCSB

12
Are We There Yet?

Abraham's Story
So Many Diamonds

Based on Genesis 22

Abraham creeps into bed beside Sarah's sleeping figure. He can't stop the trembling as he recalls the events of the day.

> *His final, broken prayer: "Please—I trust—he was never mine—always Your gift—but Sarah—bring him back or else kill me, too—"*
>
> *His own hand, raised and shaking above Isaac, precious boy of promise.*
>
> *Sharp knife, glinting bright sun.*
>
> *Isaac's eyes, widening in disbelief, terror, confusion, but still—somehow—trust. Love. Those eyes he still remembers blinking up from Sarah's arms that first beautiful morning. Sarah's laughter, rich and ringing, hour after hour, day after day.*
>
> *Abraham's other hand coming down gentle over Isaac's eyes. Closing them himself this last time.*
>
> *His own anguished cry. Knife slashing down.*
>
> *Then the voice, thundering from heaven: "Abraham! Abraham!"*

If Sarah finds out, she will kill him.

The knife will fly once more, and no voice from heaven will stop it from piercing Abraham's heart.

Fear gives way to the manic laughter of relief. Sarah can never know. Even if he survived her wrath, she would never forgive. He would never sleep in her bed, this bed, again.

He can't stop laughing, crying, quivering. If his noise wakes her, she will have questions. He eases out of bed, out of the tent, breathes night sky.

Heaven's canopy sparkles overhead, cloudless and clean. He counts stars, so many diamonds.

> *"I swear by myself that because you have done this and have not withheld your son, your only son, I will surely bless you and make your descendants as numerous as the stars in the sky and as the sand on the seashore."*

Abraham has always believed. Past reason, past possible.

Now he believes more.

He turns and smiles on Sarah's tent, picturing her small form breathing quiet beneath blankets, right where he left her. The sweet sleep of a happy mother with a full heart.

Faithful God was. Faithful God is. Faithful God will always be.

He walks, past tent after tent after tent, his kingdom.

> *"Your descendants will take possession of the cities of their enemies, and through your offspring all nations on earth will be blessed, because you have obeyed me."*

He never thought he would say it, but he has found joy here in these tents. Heard little-boy giggles at last, savored the laughter of a wife who swore she would never laugh again. His favorite sound in the world, it never gets old.

One day these tents will be Isaac's.

> *With trembling hands he pulls the ram from the thicket, draws the knife quick across its pulsing throat. Weeps as blood seeps—thank God it isn't Isaac's—lights a fire. Arm around Isaac, he renames*

the mountain: The Lord Will Provide.

Tired at last, Abraham tiptoes back to his place at Sarah's side, mind filled with thoughts of his son's future once again. Now he knows Isaac *will* have a future, a long and fruitful one. Abraham won't see it all with his aging eyes, but he sees it by faith. Isaac will become a great nation. Abraham grins at the thought.

Kicking off sandals, he folds his legs up into Sarah's bed. She wakes and scoots closer. "Good trip?" she whispers.

"The best," he says, kissing her hair.

"In the morning, we have to talk about finding a wife for Isaac," she says. "It will be time before you know it."

"The Lord will provide," Abraham says, blinking long and slow, feeling sleep's pull. "He always provides."

Sarah chuckles and props up on one elbow, her gray braid dangling. "And will the Lord also provide a home—the kind with walls and floors—for our son and his bride? Did He mention *that* in any of these elaborate promises He only seems to proclaim when you're alone?"

Abraham brushes knuckles soft against her wrinkled cheek. His sleepy words come slow. "What can I say? Last time you overheard His promise, you laughed at Him, so. . .I'm afraid you blew your chance."

Sarah smacks him on the shoulder.

"I think Isaac *will* settle down, love, in the land the Lord has promised us. In houses. With walls and floors." He pauses, gazes with surprising affection around the darkened tent. "But you know, I've come to like this life, these tents."

Sarah harrumphs and plops back down onto her pillow.

After a long silence, a small, muffled voice says, "They've grown on me, too."

Abraham pushes up on his own elbow and grins down at her, mock shock in his voice. "Wait, are these ancient ears playing tricks? Are you saying that you—*you*—can be content, even without the home you've been begging for all these years?" He tugs on her braid.

Sarah's exaggerated sigh turns to giggles, girlish and free. She winks up at him. "I'm saying. . .I can wait."

∞

I have camped exactly one night in my life, and it was everything I imagined: fun during the day, torture at night. Our tent smelled like mildew and Cheetos, campfire and feet. All night the baby coughed and the hubby snored a duet with the guy in the tent "next door."

Rain sprinkled all night. Of course my monthly friend was wreaking havoc on my feminine region, which meant I had to get up several times to squelch across camp through rain, flashlight in one hand, tampon in the other, to the "bathroom." (That nasty place does not deserve such a lofty title as *bathroom*. A generous title would be "toilet shack," though personally, I would dub it "the tarantula-infested open-air pot"—a pot that stopped flushing somewhere around 3:00 a.m. I should know. At 3:00 a.m. I was awake, negotiating with the toilet: "Please, please, for the love of all that is holy, *flush!*")

Lord willing, I will never camp again.

I do not like to tent and camp. I do not like them, Sam I Am.

But it's more than that: I do not like temporary. I do not like uncertain. I do not like uncomfortable.

No wonder I have such a hard time with waiting.

Good thing I'm not married to Abraham. He left his home—the kind with floors and walls—and his father's family, the life he had known, and followed God. . .*somewhere*. He spent much of his life in tents, roaming place to place, never feeling settled. (And let us remember that he and his wife Sarah were *also* suffering through infertility. *Oy.*)

We have reached the final chapter of this book, but chances are you haven't reached the final chapter of your wait. Chances are you are still journeying through the in-between places, living in tents. Every day you ask God, "Are we there yet?"

One day, friend, you will get there.

There might not be where you wanted or where you expected, but there you will be. One day this wait will end. Eventually you are going to get some kind of resolution.

So how do we prepare ourselves to handle God's answers when they come?

When God Says, "Surprise!"

As of this writing, there is something wonky with Google Maps. If you type in "Mount Rushmore, South Dakota," Google Maps takes you. . .not to Mount Rushmore. It takes you to Storm Mountain Center, a Methodist campsite and retreat twelve miles away. So many tourists have ended up there, lost and confused, that the center's parking lot now displays a sign: "Your GPS is wrong. This is *not* Mount Rushmore."[1]

Sometimes life works that way. We're waiting, we're traveling, and we *think* we know where we are headed, but—*surprise!*—we end up somewhere else. If you had told me six years ago that I'd spend the next five years in coastal North Carolina planting a church and writing Christian books for women, I would have either laugh-cried or fallen over in shock (probably both). But this is where God's GPS has directed us, and what a great adventure it has been!

If you had told my friend Marni that her baby delay would result in her having two beautiful babies, six months apart—one adopted, one a surprise of her own—well, I bet she would have taken an extremely long nap, an even longer "babymoon," and started stockpiling diapers!

If you had told my friend Carmen that one day she would be half joking with her husband, Alex, that it might be fun to move somewhere else, go support a small church—and less than a month later Alex would have a new job and they'd own a house down the road from me, helping me and my husband with our church planting. . .she might not have told the joke in the first place.

Of course, God's GPS for our lives isn't faulty. It hasn't been programmed wrong. When we take unexpected detours, they may be unexpected to us, but they are not a shock to God. He isn't sitting up in heaven, face in His palm, whispering to Jesus, *"Whoops! Didn't see that coming! My bad!"*

Certainly our own choices, and even other people's choices, can sometimes send us on a detour God hadn't necessarily wanted us to take. But *even then*, Romans 8:28 assures us that our powerful God can take bad choices, foolish decisions, even sin—and bring good out of the mess: "In all things God works for the good of those who love him, who have been called according to his purpose." In all things— surprising detours, lengthy delays—God, who saw them coming, can bring good.

When God Says No

In chapter 10 I started telling the story of Kevin's disappointing junior year in football, still a tender topic—let us henceforth refer to it as "the Scout Team Incident."

Two years later, after a second year of being overlooked and underused, Kevin decided to give up his last year of eligibility. We were getting married and going into the ministry, so why hang around wasting time on a practice squad when there were souls to save?

Three weeks before our wedding, the phone rang. It was the new coach of Kevin's team.

> New coach: Kevin, we want you back.
>
> Kevin (*choking*): What?
>
> New coach: Our freshman quarterback is academically ineligible, and we need you.
>
> Kevin: Um. . .I'm about to get married. I'm about to start a new job.
>
> New coach: I know, but we need you.
>
> Kevin: Will you actually give me a chance to play? I don't want to rearrange my life if I'm just going to ride the bench without a shot at the starting job.
>
> New coach: I'll give all three quarterbacks an equal look. You'll get every third rep.
>
> Kevin: Let me ask Elizabeth. (*Hangs up, calls me [lots of happy screaming], makes a flurry of arrangements canceling our entire life, calls new coach back.*) I'm in.

So just like that, in a matter of days, we turned our whole life upside down. We delayed Kevin's graduation, postponed jobs, canceled half our honeymoon, rented an apartment—did everything it took to give his football dream one last shot.

See what God is doing? we thought. *God has been preparing this crazy happy ending for Kevin all these years.* It felt like a movie. *Cinderella* in cleats.

Kevin had a great summer practicing with the team. He had to make up for missing spring ball, but make it up he did: studied long, worked hard, stayed late. Got to know the new coach, learned his system. When the first game rolled around, the coach started another guy but said he would make good on his promise. He planned to give all three players a shot to start, one by one, and then he would pick a starting quarterback for the rest of the season.

Third game, Kevin finally got his turn: After five years, he was going to start as quarterback for the first time in his college career. It was all over the local news and the school paper, the story of the fifth-year player who came back. Who never gave up.

Our families were freaking out. Our church was freaking out. A million friends bought tickets to the game.

We prayed our hearts out for days. After so many years of waiting and working and praying, even through the Scout Team Incident, surely God was going to give Kevin one of those epic the-underdog-gets-the-win sports moments. They would be making a movie out of it later—there would be *Rudy*, and there would be *Kevin*.

First series: Kevin (my husband! I'm married to the quarterback! I'm Mrs. Letterman Jacket!) runs onto the field. I scream so loud I lose my voice. Both our mothers nearly faint with excitement. But the defense seems to read the offense's mind, and they stop every play.

Second series: Kevin runs back onto the field. I find more voice and scream some more. Again the defense pushes them backward.

Third series: Kevin runs back onto the field. With no voice left to scream, I nearly claw my mother-in-law's arm off. Kevin makes a couple of decent passes, but the defense stops them again.

The coach pulls Kevin out of the game halfway through the first quarter.

He doesn't go back in.

He never really got a chance.

I sit stunned in the stands, leaking tears for the rest of the game, brokenhearted for my new husband who has fought so hard, kept a great attitude, honored God, and now been passed over again. I can see his pain in the way he stands, the slump in his shoulders. My heart rends, watching him cheer and butt slap the other quarterbacks, even as I know he is dying inside.

After the most agonizing three quarters of a football game ever in the history of football games, I wait in our car outside the locker room. Kevin doesn't say a word, just gets in and starts crying on the steering wheel. We sit in the Avenger—the car we fell in love in, the car he drove me to church in all those years—and cry together.

The rest of the season is a disappointing blur. Kevin doesn't start the next game or the next. He has a few amazing moments, like when he leads the team to outscore the number one team in the country 25 to 7 for two quarters, and when he starts one more game late in the season—but all in all he doesn't get the glorious success we had been hoping for. Begging for. Expecting God to give.

Sometimes we wait and pray and work and do all the things we are supposed to do, and maybe for a while it looks like we are going to get our way, but we don't.

Does that mean the time is lost? That we did something wrong?

I say no.

Those long heartbreaking years of working in obscurity, cheering other people on, and serving when he felt mistreated and abused made Kevin a noble man. A humble man. A great man. The greatest man I have ever met.

Those years helped him fall more in love with ministry than with football.

Those years made him the husband he is, the father he is, the friend he is, the minister he is, the man of God he is.

God said no, and it's not like we look back on that answer and jump around cheering and high-fiving—it's still a sad memory, a disappointment, a scar—but God's wisdom is clear. God knew Kevin. God knew what He was doing.

Never forget this: Our suffering becomes our story. God's *nos* are as much a part of our testimony as His *yeses*.

God said no to Abraham ever settling down in a permanent home but said yes to a son with his beloved wife, Sarah. Abraham lived long enough to see his son happily married to a God-fearing woman, Rebekah. After Sarah's death, Abraham remarried and had six other children. The Bible says that at the end of his life, "Abraham was now very old, and the LORD had blessed him in every way" (Genesis 24:1).

If you are struggling over a *no* from God, here are a few tips:

Give yourself permission, and time, to grieve. It's not wrong to be sad, to mourn the loss of something (or someone) you wanted. Feeling sad doesn't mean you don't trust God or that you are rebelling against His will for your life. Feeling sad means you are a human with feelings—feelings God designed you to have.

In time the pain should fade as the wound heals. You may always have a scar, but one day it won't hurt as much—maybe not at all—when you touch it.

Don't pull away from God when you are sad. He still wants to comfort you even when He doesn't give you what you want. (Remember, *no* isn't a punishment from God or a sign of His anger.)

Let your no *remind you not to seek heaven on earth.* Here in this fallen world, we all live with holes in our hearts: people lost, dreams broken, blessings missing. Let disappointment and sorrow point you to the joy that lies ahead, the days when God Himself will dry our tears (Isaiah 25:8; Revelation 21:4).

Don't let stubbornness destroy the life you do have. As Solomon says, there is "a time to weep. . .a time to mourn. . .a time to search and a time to give up" (Ecclesiastes 3:4, 6). There may come a time when you have to (or choose to) forfeit the search, give up the wait. Take the time you need to weep and grieve. One day, when your heart has begun to mend, the time will also come to get up again. I pray that you find the strength to move forward, the courage to choose joy, the wisdom not to live in the land of "what might have been," and the flexibility it takes to decide to love the life you *already have*.

Dare to imagine a different life. Pray that God plants a new dream in your heart. In time, my friend, as hard as it may be to imagine today, *He will.* Like Abraham and Sarah, you can find joy, even laughter, in the end. Home in tents.

As God restored the fortunes of His people after a long and painful journey, after terrible loss, so can He resurrect your dreams and revive your joy:

> *When the Lord restored the fortunes of Zion,*
> *we were like those who dreamed.*
> *Our mouths were filled with laughter,*
> *our tongues with songs of joy.*
> *Then it was said among the nations,*
> *"The Lord has done great things for them."*
> *The Lord has done great things for us,*
> *and we are filled with joy.*
>
> *Restore our fortunes, Lord,*
> *like streams in the Negev.*
> *Those who sow with tears*
> *will reap with songs of joy.*
> *Those who go out weeping,*
> *carrying seed to sow,*
> *will return with songs of joy,*
> *carrying sheaves with them.*

Psalm 126

When God Says Yes

I share this next story with great joy but also with some anxiety. Anxiety because I realize many of you reading this book still ache in the throes of infertility, and I don't want to share a story that adds to your pain. I know how tormented I have been by other people's "Listen to how God answered my pregnancy prayers" stories. I don't know why God says yes to some people and no or "keep waiting" to others; I don't understand why I got a *yes* to my baby-wait when some friends have not. I also understand that my wait wasn't as long as that of some others—for us it felt like an eternity, but others have suffered longer.

This is my story, my testimony. My God-with-His-arms-around-me-before-the-tomb story. God made me a storyteller, and I am bound to share what stories He gives. If you choose to read, I hope this story brings not more heartache, but hope and healing.

By December of 2004, we had prayed thousands of prayers begging God to give us a child. I'd begged, bargained, blown up. Many nights I woke in the night and soaked my pillow with tears, praying till dawn.

On Christmas night, 2004, I was just relieved at having survived the day. There had been no children, no Santa, no visions of sugarplums dancing in little heads. Somehow I had made it through without a meltdown and had even managed to enjoy the holiday for what it was, a special time with family: husband, parents, three grown siblings, new sister-in-law.

As the night drew to a close, my father, who had been a preacher for more than forty years, gathered our family together. We recounted blessings from the past year, talked of dreams for the future. Every family member wished for the same thing: a baby by the following Christmas. We shed tears, and as the hour grew late, Dad ended our Christmas by inviting us all to pray for the coming year. Around the circle we went, each of us begging God in turn, "Please, by this time next year, give Kevin and Elizabeth a baby." My family had prayed for us to have a baby for a long time, but never quite like this: united as a family, all in one room, echoing a single plea—"by this time next year."

A few months later, Kevin and I began seeing a new specialist who had fresh ideas. That spring, the faintest of lines on a pregnancy test made us scream and cry and dance in the bathroom at midnight, and then panic, because maybe we don't know how to read these tests, and chug more water, and sprint to the grocery store at

1:00 a.m. to buy another test, a digital one that *said the word*, just to be absolutely positively no-way-it's-a-misfire sure: I was pregnant! I embraced the months of exhaustion and nausea with ecstatic gratitude. Every time I hung my head over the trash can, I was singing inside.

The baby was due December 18. All through my pregnancy, people teased me: "A Christmas baby, how terrible!" But I, in my first-pregnancy naïveté, was convinced that the baby would come early so I could recover from the delivery in plenty of time for Christmas. We had waited so long to get pregnant; surely we wouldn't have to wait past our due date to meet our child.

But December 18 came and went, and the baby only seemed to settle deeper into my womb. December 19, December 20, December 21—nothing. Not a single useful contraction. As Christmas Day loomed, I began to despair.

I was never going to have this baby.

I had prayed so long to get pregnant, now I'd be the only pregnant woman who stayed that way forever.

But wouldn't you know? Cassidy Joy Thompson entered the world—seven pounds five ounces of answered prayer—on Christmas night, 2005, at 9:46 p.m.

But we didn't get it right away.

It was several weeks before my mother suddenly turned to me, tears brimming, and breathed, "Do you remember our prayer last Christmas night?" And we realized that Cassidy Joy had been born, *to the minute*, one year after my family had begged God, "By this time next year, please give us a child."

I don't know why God chose to answer *that* prayer with *that* timing, but this I know: our Christmas miracle healed many things in my heart that had been wounded through our long baby-wait. It was as if God went out of His way to show me, *"See, Elizabeth? All those prayers you thought I was ignoring? I was just waiting for My big reveal. You're a writer, so I gave you a story. Now get out there and tell it."*

And that leads me to something we have to talk about: What will you do if God says yes? Will you think, *Finally! I'm so glad that's over!*

and move on with your life? As you enjoy the gift, will you remember the Giver?

When we get *yeses* from God, like the leper Jesus healed—one of ten blessed men—let us remember to come stumbling back to fall on our knees, thanking God (Luke 17:11–19). Let us not keep our stories to ourselves but share our gratitude with anyone who will listen. Let us turn back, time and again, to praise and to thank the Lord. Let us shout the psalmist's words of celebration in Psalm 66:

> *Come and hear, all you who fear God;*
> *let me tell you what he has done for me. . . .*
> *God has surely listened*
> *and has heard my prayer.*
> *Praise be to God,*
> *who has not rejected my prayer*
> *or withheld his love from me!*
>
> PSALM 66:16, 19–20

I tell anyone who will listen the story of my Cassidy's miracle birth. *I can't keep it to myself.* Cassidy's birth, Cassidy's life, remind me of the faithfulness of God: His attention to detail, His wondrous sense of humor.

Cassidy is my Isaac. Her story makes me weep with joy and laugh with God.

When God Says, "Wait Some More"

Right now I'm waiting on half a dozen major life things. Things Kevin and I have spent years praying about, daring to dream, working toward.

I wait for the day my children, my four precious miracles, give their lives to God. Daily I pray that God helps us help Him shape their faith, win their hearts. I pray for the people they marry, that even now God protects and shapes my future kids-in-law.

I have two novels sitting on my computer's hard drive, waiting to find a home with publishers. They are the best work I can offer, my heart and soul in story form. I have devoted at least four years to each one—thousands of hours of life—and I'm still tweaking. Still revising. Still waiting. Still wondering if I will ever get to publish mainstream novels for tweens and teens, the way I have wanted to for thirteen years. Time and again I have joked with God: "You know, God, I realize that to You a thousand years are like a day and all, but to me, thirteen years is a *stinking long time*. Sorry for shouting. I'm just saying." *Sighhhhhhhh.*

And that's not all. In my garage, I have a rug. A hand-sewn rug from India, special ordered to coordinate with our couches, pillows, and curtains. When we ordered it, it was a rare splurge, a gift from my husband.

I have only seen the rug twice, for five minutes.

Now it stands, rolled up, in a dusty corner of my garage, still in its original packaging. It has stood there four years.

Six years ago we moved into our dream home, a home we never could have afforded in normal times. The housing market had crashed, the house went into foreclosure, and we ended up as the shocked and unlikely beneficiaries of a market gone wrong.

Pinching ourselves, feeling spoiled rotten by God, we moved in with our three littles. (Our very first night in the new house, our son broke it in by vomiting on the carpet. At the time we joked it was a good omen, a sign this was truly home.) For the first time in years—maybe ever—I let my heart relax and feel safe: We were settled. We were never leaving this place, these people. For the first time in my life, I could call a city my permanent home, stop living with the shadow of fear clouding my life, the fear that we might move at any given moment.

The house had been neglected and abused, so we set about renovating and repairing. For months we lived in dust and disorder, but since Kevin and I are putterers and tinkerers, we loved the whole process.

We bought couches and ordered the rug the next January. Delivery was promised within four to six months.

In the meantime, now that we had finally found the house we

planned to grow old and die in, we started praying and trying for a fourth child (we who never thought we'd have even one). My parents moved into our basement during a time of transition in their careers, and we spent every night discussing their options. After several months, I finally got pregnant and was happily throwing up in every trash can I could find—I hadn't forgotten the anguish of infertility, so I treasured the misery. Besides, everyone said intense nausea was a sign of a strong pregnancy, something to be grateful for. The rug still hadn't arrived, but we were too busy throwing up, getting settled, and chasing three littles around to even notice.

And in a matter of three weeks, the life we had known fell to pieces.

After a chaotic nine-month roller-coaster ride of crazy options, my parents announced their decision to move far, far away. A few days later, my husband told me his employer could no longer afford his salary, and we would also have to move—leave family, friends, home, everything. In three weeks, all of us would be moving out of our house, all at the same time.

Moving week arrived, as did the date of our first ultrasound. As I lay there on the table, fighting the constant nausea, scanning the room for a trash can, the chatty ultrasound tech got quiet. Too quiet, too long. I reached for Kevin's hand. My eyes frantically combed the fuzzy black-and-white screen, searching for the happy flicker of a healthy heartbeat. There was the precious little peanut shape—there the head; there the two tiny nubs that would grow into arms; there a tiny spot, the baby's heart—but the heart lay still. It did not beat.

There are no words for such grief.

I spent the next days in a fog of despair, bleeding out hope on a blanket on one of our new couches. Watching as my parents moved out of my house and friends quietly packed our life into boxes because I couldn't do it myself.

Still bleeding, still dying, we moved. We stuck a FOR RENT sign in the front yard of our dream house and left. My parents drove in one direction, we in another.

The rug had still not arrived.

We spent eleven months living "in between"—temporary house, temporary job, preparing to move to a different city within the year to plant a new church. In the tenth month, the doorbell rang. The mailman stood on the doorstep, balancing a ten-foot-tall, rolled-up package against his shoulder. A handcrafted rug for a house we no longer lived in, for a life we no longer led.

I couldn't even open it. That rug felt like a cruel taunt, a reminder of what might have been. All we had planned, all we had lost.

We tucked it in a corner of the garage. A few months later, we moved again, taking the still-unopened rug with us to our next rental house. There would be no place for it in our small, carpeted living room, so the rug stayed in its wrapping in a corner of the garage.

After two years, Kevin opened the rug without me knowing. Unwrapped it, unfurled it, laid it out on the driveway in all its glory. Called me out to see. It was even more beautiful than I'd remembered. He took pictures, wanting to put it up for sale online.

I refused.

He looked at me like I was nuts: This rug had sat unopened in our garage for two years, we were still trying to claw our way out of debt incurred from the unexpected moves and medical expenses, needing every dollar we could scrape together, and I still wanted to keep the rug?

I couldn't explain why, but I couldn't do it. Couldn't let go. Kevin thought I was crazy, but he, having great respect for my crazy after all these years, humored me for another year. He unwrapped it again the next summer; my answer was still no.

Another year passed. A rich year, all kindergarten and potty training and new friends.

And now here we are, present tense. Last week I was out in our garage, searching for a lost toy, when I brushed up against the rug again. Still rolled up, still in its original packaging. For the first time in four years, when I saw it, it didn't fill me with pain. Didn't feel like a reminder of the place we'd lost, the people we miss, the lives that might have been.

Now that rug feels like a promise of things still to come. A future that isn't here yet but that I can almost see winking at us just around the bend. The promise of finally feeling settled after a long season of wandering. The hope of one day owning our own home again. Doing the things people do when they are settled: hanging pictures, building swing sets, planting perennials.

I'm still waiting to unwrap that rug a third and final time. Sometimes I talk to God about it, reminding Him that we have a dream in our hearts left unfulfilled. He once gave us the gift of a home we loved—a sense of security and permanence—but the permanence turned out to be mere mirage, and we did not stay long enough to enjoy it.

For the past five years, we have found peace and contentment in borrowed houses, our "tents": We have raised kids, healed from loss, had a fourth (really a fifth) baby. We have loved hard and laughed long. We have been happy, but we haven't been *home*. I ask God, if He is willing, to give us a home of our own again someday soon. It doesn't have to be big or fancy or the house of our dreams—just a house of our own, with room for a rug.

Still Waiting? God Gets It.

What will your story be?

I pray that you keep praying.

Keep resisting the pitfalls.

Keep clinging to faith and to friends.

Keep choosing joy on your journey, wherever it leads.

I love these lines from Hebrews 11, the famous passage celebrating men and women of faith:

> *All these people were still living by faith when they died. They did not receive the things promised; they only saw them and welcomed them from a distance.*
>
> VERSE 13

Abraham and Sarah never left their tents, never found their

forever home. They died as tent dwellers. After Sarah's death, their son Isaac brought his bride, Rebekah, home to live in his mother's tent. Not her house. Her tent. *That* wait—the wait for stability, a permanent home—never ended, but Abraham and Sarah's wait for a child *did*. Oh, how it did! In old age they had a son. A son of promise. A son who made them laugh. A son who birthed a nation:

> *When God made a promise to Abraham, since He had*
> *no one greater to swear by, He swore by Himself:*
>
> *I will indeed bless you,*
> *and I will greatly multiply you.*
>
> *And so, after waiting patiently, Abraham obtained*
> *the promise.*
>
> HEBREWS 6:13–15 HCSB

I don't know how your wait ends, or when, but this I know, this we have seen:

God sees.

God hears.

God cares.

God feels our pain when the wait stretches long. He gets it.

God sent Jesus to earth and through His Son experienced life as we live it: all we feel, how we hurt. Now Jesus, our brother, sits in heaven, advocating on our behalf (1 John 2:1–2). And He does more than just intercede when we sin; Hebrews tells us He empathizes with us when we are tempted:

> *Now that we know what we have—Jesus, this great*
> *High Priest with ready access to God—let's not let it*
> *slip through our fingers. We don't have a priest who is*
> *out of touch with our reality. He's been through weak-*
> *ness and testing, experienced it all—all but the sin. So*
> *let's walk right up to him and get what he is so ready to*

give. Take the mercy, accept the help.

4:14–16 MSG

I picture Jesus leaning in and whispering to God, *"You see what a tough time she's having while she waits? I remember what that felt like. She's going to need some extra encouragement and Holy Spirit power to get her through this."*

During a painful time in Israel's history, as they languished in exile, God called on His people to wait for Him, offered hope for a future yet unseen. These passages transcend time and circumstance to reveal God's heart of affection and compassion for His people. He preserved these words so that you and I might also draw comfort, knowing that He hurts when we hurt, He rejoices when we rejoice:

> *Therefore,* wait for Me—
> *this is the Lord's declaration—*
> *until the day I rise up. . . .*
> *On that day it will be said to Jerusalem:*
> *"Do not fear;*
> *Zion, do not let your hands grow weak.*
> *Yahweh your God is among you,*
> *a warrior who saves.*
> *He will rejoice over you with gladness.*
> *He will bring you quietness with His love.*
> *He will delight in you with shouts of joy."*

ZEPHANIAH 3:8, 16–17 HCSB, emphasis added

Wait for Me.

Wait for the Warrior who saves, my friend.

Don't give up on God.

Don't give up too soon.

Be proactive, be persistent, but don't take matters into your own hands in sinful ways.

Wait for Me.

Do your part, all you can do, but then *let God do His.* In His own time, in His own way, God will answer.

One day He will bring quiet after all your turmoil.

Even now He delights in you, with shouts of joy.

Wait for Me.

God sees.

God hears.

God cares.

At journey's end, I pray you look back and say, "I'm better because of the wait." Better. Stronger. Closer. Humbler. More prayerful. More faithful. More confident. More compassionate. More selfless. More grateful.

At journey's end, I pray you lift hands to heaven, tears in your eyes and praise in your heart, and say, "It was worth the wait."

Waiting Room Reading

For Further Study
You can read New Testament reflections on Abraham, Sarah, and others in Hebrews 11. For more on how our earthly life is but a temporary home, a tent, read 2 Corinthians 5.

Journal Prompt
What changes is waiting accomplishing even now in your heart? How might you be different at the end of this season in your life—more pleasing to God, more like His Son—no matter the final outcome of your prayer? If God says no, can you imagine your life differently? If God says yes, how will you come back to praise Him?

Prayer Prompt
LORD, *hear my prayer;*
let my cry for help come before You.
Do not hide Your face from me in my day of trouble.
Listen closely to me;
answer me quickly when I call.

For my days vanish like smoke,
and my bones burn like a furnace.
My heart is afflicted, withered like grass;
I even forget to eat my food. . . .

But You, LORD, are enthroned forever;
Your fame endures to all generations.
You will rise up and have compassion on Zion,
for it is time to show favor to her—
the appointed time has come.
PSALM 102:1–4, 12–13 HCSB

Notes

Chapter 5. When Prayer Becomes a Battleground
  1. Ann Voskamp, *One Thousand Gifts* (Grand Rapids: Zondervan, 2010), 175.

Chapter 8. Finding Joy in the Journey
  1. This idea is adapted from a journaling practice I learned from my wonderfully insightful father (and fellow deep thinker), Sam Laing. Thanks, Dad!

Chapter 9. When Faith Starts Fading
  1. I am grateful to my friend, Bible scholar and apologist Dr. Douglas Jacoby (www.douglasjacoby.com), for helping to shape many of my views on scriptural interpretation.

Chapter 12. Are We There Yet?
  1. Randee Dawn, "Google Maps Is Directing Mount Rushmore Tourists to Camping Retreat," *Today*, April 1, 2016, www.today.com/money/google-maps-directing-mount-rushmore-tourists-camping-retreat-t83781.

About the Author

Elizabeth Laing Thompson writes at LizzyLife.com about clinging to Christ through the chaos of daily life. As a minister, speaker, and novelist, she loves finding humor in holiness and hope in heartache. She lives in North Carolina with her preacher husband and four spunky kids, and they were totally worth the wait.

IF YOU LIKED THIS BOOK, YOU'LL ALSO LIKE. . .

Choosing Real
by Bekah Jane Pogue
In *Choosing Real*, author Bekah Pogue walks with women into life's unplanned circumstances—specifically frantic schedules, pain and transition, feelings of unworthiness, loneliness, and tension. . . And she reminds them it is in these very moments that God invites us to notice, respond, and even *celebrate* how He shows up—in every little detail.

Paperback / 978-1-63409-964-6 / $14.99

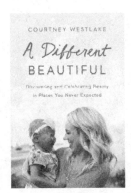

A Different Beautiful
by Courtney Westlake
In *A Different Beautiful*, Courtney explores what her family has discovered in raising a child with physical differences and what she has learned about true beauty. Through her personal insights and experiences, Courtney shares how we can all learn to find and celebrate God's version of beautiful in our lives, especially within our differences and struggles.

Paperback / 978-1-63409-726-0 / $14.99